OF UNCOMMON INTEREST

Rare early action picture of the Watford brigade galloping their steamer to a fire in 1910.
The face peering round the side is that of the engineer perched on his footplate at the rear.

Richard Whitmore

OF UNCOMMON INTEREST

True stories and photographs of
ordinary people and extraordinary events
in Victorian and Edwardian times

SPURBOOKS LIMITED

PUBLISHED BY
SPURBOOKS LTD
6 PARADE COURT
BOURNE END
BUCKINGHAMSHIRE

ISBN 0 902875 98 1

DESIGNED AND PRODUCED BY
MECHANICK EXERCISES, LONDON

MADE AND PRINTED IN GREAT BRITAIN BY
THE GARDEN CITY PRESS LIMITED
LETCHWORTH, HERTFORDSHIRE SG6 1JS

To
My father, Tom Whitmore,
and all other readers born
in the county of Hertfordshire
when Victoria was Queen,
this book is dedicated.

CONTENTS

ILLUSTRATIONS

ACKNOWLEDGEMENTS

I am greatly indebted to the following individuals and organisations for the loan of photographs and for providing the background information which enabled me to complete my researches of the stories told in this book.

THE FIREMEN AND THE FIRE
Divisional Officer Ron Percival and Mr Keith Fuller of the Hertfordshire Fire Brigade, also the brigade's former Chief Officer Geoffrey Blackstone, author of *A History of the British Fire Service*. Charles Mearing and J. J. Johnson of John Dickinson's Paper Mills, Hemel Hempstead; Alan McWhirr of Leicester; John Wild of Berkhamsted; Mrs E. C. Marsden of Gaddesden Place, Hemel Hempstead; Jessie Sansom of Whitwell; and the *Hemel Hempstead Gazette*.

THE FARM AND FARMERS
Tom Cawley, librarian Rothamsted Agricultural Research Station; Eric Brandreth, librarian Harpenden Public Library; Eric Oggelsby and Raphael Salaman of Harpenden; the late Edwin Grey, author of *Cottage Life in a Hertfordshire Village*; and Roy Darby of Luton.

THE SMALL BUSINESS—THE PERFUMERY
Miss Violet Lewis and the Reverend Richard Lewis.

THE LIFE OF THE POOR
W. G. Sansom, of The Shaftesbury Homes and Arethusa; Helen Poole, Assistant Curator, Hitchin Museum; F. John Smith of Royston; Gordon Thomson of Hitchin; Miss E. A. Latchmore of Hitchin, author of *A Venture*

of Faith; and the *Hertfordshire Express* (now part of the North Herts Gazette Newspaper series).

The Coming of the Motor Car
Gordon Davies, curator Hertford Museum; Chief Superintendent George Osborn of the Hertfordshire Constabulary and his son Neil, author of *The Story of Hertfordshire Police*; the *Luton News*; the British Museum Newspaper Library, Colindale; and the late Sir Kenneth Murchison, author of *Family Notes and Reminiscences*.

The Parson and a Rural Living
Mary Gadd, Director of Museums North Hertfordshire; and Canon Arthur Suffrin, former Vicar of St Mary's, Pirton, now of Melksham, Wilts.

The Poachers
H. S. Bonnett, Letchworth, Colin Dawes, curator of Stevenage Museum, and his assistant Rosemary Gilmour; Jack Franklin of Graveley Hall, near Stevenage; the Hertfordshire Constabulary; and the late Reginald Hine, author of *Hitchin Worthies*.

The Riot
Margaret Marshall of Watford Reference Library; Daphne Fisher of Watford; Frank Paybody, former Assistant Chief Constable of Hertfordshire; and the *Watford Observer*.

County Schooling—the Straw Plaiters
Vera Thrussell of Pirton; Marian Nichols of Luton Museum; Robert Waldock and Gordon Thomson of Hitchin.

A Public Enquiry—the Train Accidents
Albert Sheldrick, curator Ashwell Museum; F. John

14

Smith of Royston; Robert Waldock of Hitchin; the *Royston Crow* newspaper and the Historical Records Department of British Railways.

A CRAFTSMAN'S LIFE—THE WHEELWRIGHT
Kathleen and Peggy Wilson of Breachwood Green; Audrey Wadowska of Holland Park, London.

THE FORGOTTEN VISIONARY
Mrs Audrey Wadowska of Holland Park, London.

A DISASTER—THE PIONEER AVIATORS
The British Museum Newspaper Library; Bob Broeder of Syndication International Ltd., London; Stuart Fisher of Letchworth Camera Club; Alan Fleck of Hitchin Museum; and Reg Cannon of Hitchin.

THE PHOTOGRAPHERS

The early photographers of Hertfordshire, whose work is reproduced in this book, include the following:

George Avery, Hitchin; Albert Bishop, Welwyn; Robert Clark, Royston; Arthur Clutterbuck, Letchworth; P. T. Culverhouse, Hemel Hempstead; Frederick Downer, Watford; Arthur Elsden, Hertford; Percy Jacob, Royston; H. W. Lane, St Albans; T. B. and T. W. Latchmore, Hitchin; Thomas and Arthur Melbourne-Cooper, St Albans; J. Mott, Markyate; H. G. Moulden, Hitchin; J. T. Newman, Berkhamsted; H. Newton, Hertford; Frederick Thurston, Luton; H. Wilton, Stevenage.

––––––

Not surprisingly many of the original photographs taken by these men were in a poor condition, having faded and deteriorated generally over the past 60 to 110 years since the prints were made. It is a curious fact, however, that, if these old prints are copied with care, the camera will re-discover in them details which—to the human eye at least—seemed to have disappeared. Most of those selected for this book were copied for me by Alfred Cole, a photographer and colleague whose patience and skill has restored much of the original high quality to the work of his Victorian predecessors.

INTRODUCTION

Since most of the stories in this book cover events that
made national news in Victorian and Edwardian England
it is not surprising that—more than once—I have found
myself trying to imagine how they would have been
treated had they occurred in The Television Age. There's
little doubt that, because of its insatiable daily demand for
new information and fresh topics for discussion, television
would have seized upon all of them—if not for their
importance as news stories, then for general interest and
amusement. Modern communications would, for
example, have enabled cameramen and reporters to be at
the scene in plenty of time to record the astonishing street
battles and looting in Watford the night they cancelled
the coronation celebrations because King Edward VII
was seriously ill. Imagine, too, the heated studio debates
and investigations that would have followed the dis-
closure by a Board of Trade inspector that the train
disaster at Royston was caused by a quarter of a mile of
faulty track which had virtually rotted away through
neglect! The programmes concerned with exposing social
injustices would have had much to say about the child
straw-plaiters who, at the expense of their education,
could earn more money each week than their fathers did
labouring on the land; and there would have been endless
protests from the environmentalists about the arrival in
our country lanes of the motor car—particularly the one
involved in a fatal collision at twenty miles an hour
which resulted in the unfortunate chauffeur being
prosecuted for 'manslaughter by furious driving'.

Although for purely partisan reasons I have selected
stories that involved my home county of Hertfordshire,

the problems and attitudes which they illustrate existed throughout most of England at that time. What, in my opinion, makes them even more interesting is that each is fully illustrated by contemporary photographs—indeed, I would like to think that this book is as much a tribute to the work of the early news photographers of Hertfordshire as it is to the verbose but highly accurate Victorian journalists upon whose information I have relied so much during my researches. This is the first time that many of these stories have been published in full, actually accompanied by original photographs taken at the time. Since very few Victorian newspapers possessed the blockmaking equipment needed to reproduce photographs in print at short notice the photographer was normally obliged to earn his money by working through the night to produce hundreds of postcard prints which were then offered on sale to the public the following morning. The more sensational the story, the more he sold. For instance, during the three days after the great fire of Gaddesden Place, the Hemel Hempstead photographer, P. T. Culverhouse, sold more than three thousand postcard pictures of the burnt-out mansion.

It is worth recalling, too, the difficult conditions under which these early photographers worked; they had no fast cars to get them quickly to the scene, neither did they have any elaborate lightweight cameras, fast film or synchronised flashlight equipment. Some had a pony and trap, but many covered their assignments either on foot or on a bicycle, setting off with an assistant on a ten-mile journey, weighed down by the heavy wooden plate camera and tripod strapped to their backs and carrying the cumbersome wooden cases which contained the large glass plates upon which they made their exposures. There were many such men in Hertfordshire, probably two or three in each main town, which makes it all the more infuriating that such a small portion of their prolific output has survived to be appreciated today. On the other hand, their very scarcity makes the discovery of a long-forgotten print all the more exciting and a collection such as is reproduced here, all the more interesting.

My own first encounter with Victorian news items occurred within a week of beginning my career in journalism. As a junior reporter on what was then the *Hertfordshire Express*, I was assigned the weekly task of climbing into a dusty loft above the editor's office in which were stored dozens of bound volumes containing most of the weekly editions of that newspaper right back to mid-Victorian times. From the brittle pages I had to select and type out a short item of about a hundred words, which I considered gave an interesting glimpse of the very different way of life which existed in those days. This, with the editor's approval, was then reproduced at the end of 'John Quill's' gossip column under the title *75 Years Ago*. It was a job which must have rated very low on the newspaper's productivity charts, since I usually allowed it to take up most of one morning. This was not because I had difficulty in finding an item, but that I found too many, being lured from page to page by what the journalists of the day would refer to as *events of uncommon interest*. It is significant that someone on that newspaper is still doing the job today as, indeed, are young reporters on other newspapers up and down the country. Their editors know full well that this unimportant little item gives the reader a good deal of pleasure, that he enjoys the opportunity to dodge back for a moment in time and then return, thankful that diphtheria no longer wipes out whole families of children, sorry that Woodbines no longer cost a penny for ten.

The stories and photographs in this book offer a wide range of such journeys into the past, covering not only the more sensational events, but also the lives of everyday people whose names probably only ever appeared in print in the Births, Marriages and Deaths columns. Yet each offers some interesting reflections on life and attitudes in Victorian and Edwardian England which, to this generation, can be considered to be—*of uncommon interest.*

Richard Whitmore,

1975

1

THE FIREMEN AND THE FIRE

The events which form the climax to this chapter, the destruction by fire of a large country mansion and its horrific sequel, were not chosen simply for reasons of sensationalism, even though firemen were to talk about them for many years afterwards. They were chosen to illustrate the enormous problems which could confront the small and ill-equipped fire brigades upon whom most of the country relied at the turn of the century. Gaddesden Place, near Hemel Hempstead, went up in flames during the early hours of 1st February, 1905. The two main brigades which had to cope with the incident were typical of hundreds in existence at that time—one a private brigade of paid firemen, the other a group of 'gentlemen volunteers'. Their equipment, which had changed very little during the last half of the 19th century, consisted of horse-drawn pumps, operated by hand, hoses of leather or poor quality canvas and (their only effective mechanised aid) a coal-fired steamer to pump water to the scene.

The Hemel Hempstead Volunteer Fire Brigade was formed in 1845 after a town meeting, called with some urgency to discuss ways of coping with 'the spirit of incendiarism' which had made its appearance in the area. At this time, fire-raising was very common, a popular but cowardly form of revenge by disgruntled or ill-treated workers against their employers and a convenient way of delaying the progress of mechanisation which, many of the poorer classes believed, was destined to put them out of work. In 1831, for example, more than nine hundred men were convicted of setting fire to the new and hated threshing machines which were causing unemployment on the farms. This, in spite of the fact that arson was still a crime which carried the ultimate penalty. In December 1833, John Stallan of Shelford in Cambridgeshire achieved the unenviable distinction of becoming the last man in Britain to be executed for fire-raising. He confessed to starting ten fires in his village, not for the usual motive of revenge, but because he was a volunteer fireman who enjoyed his work and felt he wasn't getting enough of it! He told the judge at Cambridge Assizes that he did it for the free beer and money that went with the work.

Against this sort of background, then, the citizens of Hemel Hempstead organised their first volunteer fire-fighting force to back up the work of the only other small brigade in the district which was financed and run by an insurance company. The minutes of that inaugural meeting in 1845 record that the volunteer brigade should consist of certain *gentlemen*, who would provide uniforms and hats at their own expense, and certain *men* who would be paid for their work and would receive uniforms free of charge. In addition a number of 'pioneers' were appointed; their duty was to gallop ahead of the brigades during an alarm to locate water supplies close to the scene of the fire. These two brigades served the community until the 1880s, when the insurance company brigade was disbanded to be replaced shortly afterwards by a new one, belonging to the giant John Dickinson Paper Mills. This private brigade, formed in 1883, was the second one to feature strongly in the disaster at Gaddesden Place. It was the Dickinson brigade, too, which possessed the much envied steamer.

The steam fire engine was the most important development in fire-fighting equipment during the Victorian era. It had been invented as far back as 1829 by John Braithwaite and had put up an impressive performance at its first fire in London a year later, sending jets of water ninety feet high, into the blazing Argyll Rooms on a bitterly cold February night which had frozen all the manual pumps solid. Yet it was never adopted by any of the big city brigades; for some strange reason the chief fire officers regarded it with suspicion, some declaring it too powerful to do a proper job! Braithwaite's steamer was also much disliked by the volunteers working the manual pumps and, on several occasions when Braithwaite turned up at a big fire with his machine, the pumpers, to ensure they were going to continue in work, slashed the hoses! It was not until thirty years later that brigades finally came to acknowledge the value of the steamer which, by this time, was being produced by two London companies, Shand Mason, and Merryweathers. In 1878, Merryweathers were advertising that they had sold more than five hundred steamers to brigades up and down the country, but it was only the wealthier, private brigades such as Dickinsons, and those in the big cities, which could afford them. Dickinsons bought theirs in 1893 for £340.

It was a momentous day when a town took delivery of the first steamer. Often its arrival at the railway station was greeted by a guard of honour formed by the local firemen and other brigades from neighbouring towns. Preceded by a brass band they would pull the steamer proudly through the town to the fire station where a group of civic dignitaries would be waiting, among them some prominent local lady who had been invited to 'christen' the machine by breaking a bottle of champagne over the footplate. The names given to these steamers were often exotic; Firefly, Ajax, and Torrent. Some were christened Prince Albert, or The Victoria, the name being painted boldly in gold lettering on the side of the machine. Later, those steamers which developed any irritating faults or peculiarities while functioning at fires would be given rather less flattering names by their operators; Puffing Polly, Belching Bertha, or as on one occasion, Farting Annie. Nevertheless, whatever abuse the firemen may have heaped on their machines during the stresses of fire-fighting they were tremendously proud of them, and many brigades changed their titles from the Volunteer

Fire Brigade to the Volunteer *Steam* Fire Brigade, in
order to distinguish themselves from their less well-off
neighbours who were still working with the old manual
pumps.

The turnout of the local horse-drawn steamer was an
event which never failed to thrill children and adults
alike. For the firemen, though, it was a carefully rehearsed
procedure which varied from station to station depending
on the size of the town. In rural areas, the brigade often
had to rely not only on volunteer firemen but on volunteer
horses as well, which meant that when the alarm bell
sounded, the turnout of the steamer was always preceded
by a hell-for-leather race between the butcher, the baker,
the farmer and undertaker, each man galloping his horse
to the fire station in an endeavour to be among the first
two or three needed to make up the team and so claim
the quite substantial fee which the brigade paid for the
service. Other brigades preferred to have a regular con-
tract with a local livery stable to supply horses specially
trained for the job. With time, many of these animals
came to recognise the significance of the sound of the
alarm bell and would get very excited, anticipating the
gallop and work that lay ahead. During the latter part of
the last century, a liveryman at Ware who held the con-
tract to provide a pair of horses for the town's brigade,
had only to open his stable doors when the bell sounded,
and the horses would canter smartly round to the fire
station unaccompanied! In the bigger cities, the firemen
kept their own beasts, spending hours training them to
respond to the bell by trotting out of their stable to a
point beneath their specially designed harness which was
suspended from the ceiling by pulleys, so it could be
quickly lowered on to the animals' backs. Each harness
had an unusual split collar which dropped over the
horse's neck and was clipped together underneath.
Features such as this in the design of the equipment

enabled many brigades to turn out in less than two minutes.

The steamer itself was kept with a small gas jet burning permanently beneath the boiler, so that the water in it was kept just short of steam pressure. The fire beneath the boiler was, of course, laid ready, coal at the bottom, then sticks and finally paper on top. While the coachman and firemen were busy harnessing the horses, it was the engineer's job to run to his steps at the back of the steamer and throw a special long-burning fuse match down the funnel. The draught which resulted during the hair-raising ride was always sufficient to ensure that the boiler fire was burning well by the time the steamer arrived at the scene. Few Victorians or Edwardians ever forgot the sight of a steamer on its way to a blaze. The coachman yelling encouragement to his horses and handling them with magnificent precision along the narrow and often congested streets, the officer in charge alongside him ringing the bell and operating the handbrake where necessary, the firemen crouched in two lines along the hose box, and the engineer, clinging precariously to his handgrips, on the footplate at the rear.

By the 1870s the Fire Brigade Competitions had got into full swing and were being organised on a national scale. The principal manufacturers of the engines, Shand Mason, and Merryweathers, were offering generous prizes to the winners. One such 'friendly' contest was held at Watford in 1877 which, while providing great excitement for the huge crowd, also degenerated into a slanging match between the losers and the judges. This stemmed from the fact that most of the volunteer brigades were still very much a law unto themselves, with little regard for any national code of fire-fighting procedures which may have existed, and each quite convinced that their ideas about drill and fire-fighting techniques were the right ones. Engineer Penfold, of the Metropolitan Fire Brigade, who had the misfortune to be one of the judges

'Alice', steam pump of the Berkhamsted brigade, working to get water from a pond to a farm fire two hundred yards away, in 1912.

at this event, returned dazed to London to pen the following report to his seniors:

'I would respectfully beg that I am strongly of the opinion that these volunteer contests should find judges from their own class, as each competing brigade will always persist in following their own particular ideas, instead of following rules laid down, and will insist that their own peculiar ways are correct, and that all others are wrong and—as trickery is a great element in nearly all of them—it makes the office of judge for an impartial man a very unsatisfactory office.'

If the volunteer firemen of Victorian Hertfordshire were an arrogant race, that arrogance was merely a reflection of extreme pride in their unit. Most were tough extroverts, a dedicated élite who, usually for no money at all, were prepared to take enormous risks in what they regarded as the normal course of duty. Some brigades, in fact, charged a subscription, so that the 'gentlemen volunteers' actually paid for the privilege of putting out the

26

town's fires. Because many local authorities were slow to recognise their worth, brigades also had to rely on voluntary contributions and fund-raising events to buy their equipment. An episode at St Albans in 1899 illustrates just how much a brigade could be taken for granted and how quick the public were to criticise, when on just one occasion things went wrong.

During the evening when a fire broke out in a photographic studio in Alma Road, most members of the volunteer brigade were, it seems, scattered about various public houses in the town which, not unnaturally, were not connected to the alarm bell system. As a result the brigade was slow to turn out—very slow. According to most estimates it was something like forty-five minutes before the engine arrived at the scene, even though the street where the fire was burning was only a five-minute walk from the fire station. By this time, the studio was virtually destroyed. The incident caused an uproar which filled many columns of the local newspaper for weeks to come and set the City Council thinking seriously about whether the brigade should be taken over by the Police. The brigade captain at that time was a local ironmonger and engineer, Captain William Thorpe, who, far from being deterred by the criticism seized upon it to bring home to the citizens of St Albans the great difficulties under which their brigade was working. He pointed out that they had only been able to purchase their Merryweather steamer a few years earlier by launching an appeal.

'No one can foresee the future, no one can do impossibilities,' he wrote. 'Fires do not break out by appointment and if, as unfortunately happened in the recent case, a fire occurs at an hour when men are leaving work and seeking an hour's recreation away from home and consequently cannot be communicated with—either at their homes or places of work—delay in their arrival at the scene of the outbreak is, of necessity, bound to arise.'

27

The incident served to jerk the City Council out of its distant critical attitude; they met the firemen and together threshed out a scheme for improvements. A site for a new fire station was found and a resident caretaker employed to act also as coachman for the fire engine. In 1901 the council resolved to pay the volunteers for their services. They would in future receive 2s. od. for the first hour's work at a fire and 1s. 6d. an hour thereafter. 'St Albans,' said one city alderman, 'has a very efficient brigade and it is not fair that they should be called upon to put their hands in their own pockets to defray the expenses of their work.'

That same year, 1901, the John Dickinson Fire Brigade achieved what must then have been the goal of every dedicated fire team in the country; at the National Fire Brigades' Union camp at Basingstoke they became national champions, winning the National Steamer Drill Final in what was then an impressive record time of 35.2 seconds. In the exercise, working with a strange engine and horses, they had to make a flying start, gallop the team fifty yards, unhook the horses, connect up three fifty feet lengths of hose and hit a target with their jet. After the Duke of Marlborough had presented them with their trophy, they were invited to repeat the demonstration. They accepted, and astonished the crowd by knocking a further three seconds off the record time which they had clocked up earlier in the afternoon.

By the turn of the century the Fire Brigades' Union had done much to establish a national code of standards for firemen and this had helped to remove the undignified squabbles and scenes which had accompanied earlier competitions. There was, nevertheless, still considerable rivalry between neighbouring brigades and it was not unknown for fire to rage merrily on while the captains of the various brigades indulged in heated argument over who was to take control of the operation. It was to remove what one officer called 'these petty jealousies' that the two brigades at Hemel Hempstead, Dickinsons and the Volunteer Brigade, began to train together, organising combined drills, which in the event of a major fire would enable them to pool their resources in the most effective way possible. Their first chance to put the results of those combined drills to the test came on the night Gaddesden Place went up in flames.

The mansion which stood on a hill three miles to the north-west of Hemel Hempstead, was built in 1774 by the Halsey family, who had owned the estate for many generations. The current owner was the Right Honourable Thomas Halsey, Member of Parliament for West Hertfordshire who, at that time, was living with his family at their London home and had rented Gaddesden Place to a fellow parliamentarian, the M.P. for Preston, John Kerr. It was he, his wife and daughters, and a large corps of servants, who were in residence on the night of the fire. In retrospect, it was a fire that should never have happened. For several days the family and staff had been concerned about the strong smell of burning throughout the house, and on Tuesday 31st January, it had become so strong that the estate carpenter and other workmen were called in to try to discover the source. They examined the large boiler in the cellar and the heating pipes, but could find nothing wrong. Nobody considered it worth while to call in the fire brigade for advice; had they done so the brigade would almost certainly have discovered the smouldering beam near a boiler flue-pipe, which had been burning for days and which finally broke loose into a room in the main block of the house at 4 a.m. on 1st February.

The alarm was raised by one of the Kerr daughters and within five minutes the whole household had been alerted and evacuated outside, still in their nightclothes. One of the estate workers saddled a horse and galloped the three miles into Hemel Hempstead to sound the fire alarm. At 4.23 a.m. the brigade's horse-drawn manual pump, with

Captain Harry Hancock in charge, was on its way. 'Tele-
phonic messages' were despatched to the John Dickinson
brigade at 4.40 a.m. and they arrived at 5.30 a.m. with
Second Officer James Burles in charge. By this time, the
main block of the house was well alight. Estate workers
had formed a human chain and were desperately trying
to save the valuable contents of Thomas Halsey's library,
his paintings, antique furniture and numerous other price-
less heirlooms, but a strong wind was blowing and they
had saved only a small proportion of the contents before
the flames had surged through the corridors and engulfed
every room in the main block.

It was a hopeless task for the firemen; their only real
chance was to try to contain the fire in the main block and
save the two wings which housed the servants' quarters
and the laundry. They might have done more if they had
had a supply of water nearby but, apart from a small
domestic supply, the nearest was half a mile away in the
River Gade at the bottom of the hill. Hancock and Burles

'The flames had the
mastery . . .' This
retouched night picture
of Gaddesden Place at
the height of the fire was
said to have given an
accurate impression as the
fire engulfed the entire
main block.

put their heads together and decided to send the
Dickinson steamer down to the river to pump water up
the hill to a dam, from which the manual pumps could
then draw their water. To achieve this, the firemen laid
and connected 1,700 feet of hose between the steamer by
the river, and the house. The steamer worked perfectly
but the incline leading to the house was too great, and
when the water pressure reached 120 lb., the canvas hoses
burst. The only other source of water was from a pond on
a neighbouring estate some 2,500 feet away across a small
valley. To get this water across to the house was a
mammoth task using just about every inch of hose that
the four brigades now on the scene could supply. Incredibly, they did it. The Dickinson steamer at the pond and
then the three manual pumps from Hemel Hempstead,
Frogmore and Berkhamsted stretched across Gaddesden
Park in a relay, pumping the water from one team to the
next until it reached the hoses trained on the burning
mansion. With great difficulty they managed to provide
an erratic supply which was at least sufficient to enable
the firemen to save the two wings of the building.

The reporter from the *Hemel Hempstead Gazette* who
witnessed the event wrote: 'The flames had the mastery
and leapt higher and higher and issued from windows on
all sides of the mansion. As the dense volumes of smoke
continued to rise, and as crash after crash of windows
smashing, ceilings and floors falling through, walls crack-
ing and masonry-work tumbling, the sight was appalling
and terrible to behold. The firemen battled with the flames
until they were beaten back time and time again and, the
high wind blowing right to the inside of the building,
every room of the main block became enveloped. It was
noticed that the lead covering the coping was running
down the walls, so intense was the heat.'

During the desperate struggle to get water to the scene
there were several angry exchanges between the firemen
and the volunteers working the manual pumps. James

Burles, officer in charge of the Dickinson brigade, referred in his report to 'the disgraceful behaviour of the pumpers, bringing discredit to the various brigades', by failing to keep up a steady supply of water. Finding men to work the pumps was obviously more difficult in a remote country area like Gaddesden, than in a town where there were always plenty of volunteers eager for the 1s. 0d. an hour normally paid to the pumpers. It was exhausting work, the teams rarely able to work efficiently for more than five minutes at a stretch. Twenty-four men were needed to operate each pump (twelve on each side) with a second team of the same number standing by to relieve them. On this occasion there were not enough men to make up a relief team which meant that on several occasions during critical periods when the fire was at its height, the pumpers collapsed from exhaustion and the supply of water to the hoses stopped.

The firemen had to work on the building throughout the whole of Wednesday dealing with sporadic outbreaks which threatened the wings of the burnt-out mansion, but by the evening the situation was considered well under control. Two of the brigades were stood down, leaving the Hemel Hempstead and Dickinson brigades on duty. Hundreds of sightseers had come and gone and even the firemen and estate workers were beginning to relax when, belatedly and at one horrifying stroke, the fire reached out and snatched two victims.

William Paton, aged 45, had been butler to the Kerr family for only a few days and had spent the previous twelve hours worrying about the safety of the large store of wine in the cellars beneath Gaddesden Place. At the height of the fire he had organised a chain of staff to remove most of the cases from the cellar to the safety of the garden. Later on, worried about the possibility of looting after dusk, and when it seemed there was no danger of the fire reaching the cellar, he decided to have them replaced. He told his employer of his decision and

Mr Kerr warned him: 'Don't take any unnecessary risks. Lose all the wine rather than a life.' Paton, however, went ahead and all the cases were returned to the cellar.

With all the wine replaced, the butler was standing in the vaults with four other men—his footman James Jones, aged 21, a fireman Sidney Clark, P.C. Limbrick and an elderly helper, Alfred Dolt. Suddenly, a beam in one of the main walls burst into flames. The butler turned to the fireman with a look of alarm on his face.

'What do you think of that lot?' he asked. 'Is it safe?'

Fireman Clark assured him that it was not, and so, for the second time, the butler decided to move all the wine out. He ordered Jones the footman to go for help to move the wine cases again, but before the young man could take a step there was a deafening crash.

Paton was heard to scream 'My God!' and the next moment was buried beneath several feet of red-hot bricks as one of the main walls of the building above them crashed through the cellar roof. When his body was eventually dug out of the rubble the next morning it was burned beyond recognition—the only consolation that could be offered by the surgeon who examined the corpse was that William Paton had died instantaneously, his neck broken by the weight of the falling masonry. James Jones, the footman, was not accorded such a merciful end. As the bricks cascaded into the cellar he was thrown, still upright, into a corner where he stood pinned up to his shoulders by the hot rubble. The other three, caught only by the extremities of the collapse, managed to stagger from the cellar for help. It was dark by this time but the rescuers, with a lantern and guided by the agonised cries of 'Help me—I'm burning!' quickly located the young man in the thick dust and confusion of the cellar. Red-hot ashes were falling on his head, the only part of him that was visible above the bricks. While Captain Hancock played a hose on the rubble to try and cool it, others set to work with pick and shovel, ignoring the danger of a possible further collapse above them. It took them forty-five minutes to free the victim, James Jones remaining conscious throughout the ordeal and pleading with his rescuers to try to save the butler. The rescuers, however, knew that was pointless. The footman was eventually released and taken to hospital, but his burns were so severe that he was not expected to survive the shock and died the following morning as the firemen returned to the mansion to begin their long search for the body of the butler.

The following week, after an inquest, when the jury returned verdicts of 'accidental death' on the two victims, the volunteer firemen of Hemel Hempstead held an emergency meeting at the Swan Hotel. Captain Hancock made a forthright statement about shortcomings which the Gaddesden Place fire, the most serious in the history of their brigade, had brought to light. Unlike his opposite number in charge of the Dickinson brigade he did not level criticism at the pumpers who, he said, had worked until they could work no more. He blamed their out-of-date equipment and said the time had come when the people of Hemel Hempstead should seriously consider providing the town with a steam engine. The Town Council had been approached before about this and also about providing a new fire station but according to Captain Hancock, 'While promises have been made, nothing has been done.'

Captain Hancock's remarks found their way home. Both the council and private individuals responded quickly and in the following year, 1906, the foundation stone was laid for a new fire station and a public appeal launched to buy the Hemel Hempstead brigade their first steamer. Although they were late in getting one, they were by no means the last, for the old horse-drawn steamer took a long time dying. The first self-propelled motor fire engines may have appeared, but they caught on very slowly indeed, particularly since some of them couldn't travel as fast as a well managed horse-drawn steamer! In addition, many brigades displayed an attitude similar to their predecessors in mid-Victorian times who had been convinced that steam pumps would never replace the old manuals. Mechanical transport, they believed, was a passing fad and the horse would never be dispensed with. Consequently, it was not until the Great War that the thrilling spectacle of the old horse-drawn steamer finally began to disappear from the towns and villages of Britain.

2

THE FARM AND FARMERS

The man who plodded up the lane towards the big farm
was little more than five feet tall but his physique was
sturdy. His hair was cut short and, although clean-
shaven about the mouth, he had a fringe of whiskers
running down each side of his face to meet under the chin.
He wore a shirt with no collar and thick brown corduroy
trousers held up by braces. Tied loosely around his neck
was a red neckerchief, the ends of which were knotted to
his braces where they passed over the shoulder. The
corduroys were lifted slightly above the ankles by means
of a short leather strap fastened around each trouser leg
just below the knee.

His christian name could have been any one of a score
taken from the Old Testament; David, Noah, Eli,
Jeremiah, even Moses, but he was most probably known
by a nickname; Wacky Russell, Clipper Weston, Slappy
Twidell or Pincher Smith, given to him in fun when he
was a boy and staying with him for life. There was
a good chance, too, that his life would be a long one,
for the Hertfordshire farm labourer of the mid-19th
century was, on average, remarkably healthy despite the
privations he had to endure.

In summer, he rose at 4 a.m. and did an hour's work
in his little cottage garden before breakfast, because the
products of his garden would make an important contribution towards the survival of his family during the
coming winter. His cottage was one of a cluster of eight.
It had two rooms upstairs and two down and the rent was
1s. 6d. a week. The floor at ground level consisted of
bricks set into the soil foundations and the only covering
was a thin strip of coconut matting and a clean corn sack

for a hearth rug. He had six children, the youngest of which slept with him and his wife in the tiny back bedroom. Of the five others who occupied the second bedroom, the two girls slept in one bed and the three boys in the other—the sexes kept apart by an old curtain that hung down from the ceiling.

The home had no sinks, no running water and no drains. The family shared a communal well with the occupants of the seven other cottages, and the household refuse was thrown into the 'dung'll hole'—a round hole about three feet deep which was to be found at the bottom of every cottage garden. The rotting refuse from this pit was later used as garden fertiliser. The eight families also shared a solitary earth closet, the privy, taking turns to empty and clean it. To do this, they first dug a trench well away from the cottages before removing the contents of the closet with a long-handled scoop and transporting it in pails to the trench, which was immediately filled in. It was an operation usually performed discreetly late at night; the farm workers considered themselves more fortunate than the many cottagers, living in the centre of the village, who had no gardens and were obliged to employ the services of the old man with his stinking night soil cart—commonly referred to as 'the parish tackle'.

The coming month was an important one for the farm labourer; it was harvest time and, although the hours were long and tiring, it meant that his weekly wage of 13s. od. would be supplemented at the end of the month by a bonus of perhaps £2 or £3. This would buy new clothing for his wife and some of the children and possibly some new boots for himself. The boots the man wore that day on his way to the fields were a treasured possession, being stout-soled, well-studded and with metal-tipped heels and toes. He examined and maintained his boots regularly, carefully replacing any missing nails or tips and greasing them heavily during bad weather so that the leather would keep soft and supple. Like many others, he often lined the soles with soft hay, which acted as an absorbent and made the boots more comfortable.

After a walk of nearly two miles from his cottage, the labourer reached the field where he and his colleagues were due to start harvesting, at 6 a.m. Some of the older labourers wore the traditional round smocks, made of dark green material with coloured beads worked into the smocking across the chest. The men who still favoured smocks usually owned two, one of which was kept for Sundays; those who could afford only one would wear it all week and then turn it inside-out for church or chapel on the Sabbath. Although horse-drawn cutters were in use on some farms, much of the harvesting was still done by hand with the reaping hook and scythe. The work was hot and back-breaking with the scythe-men working across a field in one or two rows taking their time from the 'Lord', or leader, at the head of each row, the broad-bladed scythes singing in rhythm as they were swung in regular time through the wheat and barley.

Hay-making group at Codicote Lodge Farm, near Welwyn, about 1890.

After perhaps five hours a lunch-break, or 'beaver time' was more than welcome. The beer was provided free by the farmer but the men brought their own food with them in small baskets of plaited rush. All ate with the aid of a pocket knife in what was termed the 'thumb-bit' method. A doorstep slice of bread, held in the left hand, on to which was placed either a slice of salted pork, or cheese, or bloater, held in position by the thumb. To this was added a slice of vegetable and a final wedge of bread. The pocket knife was then used to cut off the piece protruding beyond the thumb, which being held between the knife blade and right-hand thumb, was taken to the mouth.

While the labourer was in the fields, his wife had plenty to do at home. Since few cottages had ovens, nearly all her food had to be boiled in the large pot which hung from a bar in the chimney over the living room fire. She normally cooked twice a week, on Wednesdays and Sundays, making meat puddings from inferior cuts of pork or beef; the vegetables were boiled at the same time, kept separate in net bags. On Sunday the pot had to be cleaned out quickly to be ready for boiling the family's clothes on wash-day the following morning.

The wife was usually responsible for the feeding and welfare of the family pig. If those in each community were too poor to keep one individually, they shared one, and the day it was killed was something of an event. The women were up early boiling gallons of water in readiness for the arrival of the slaughterman with his knives, rack and scalding tub. The killing itself was a noisy and bloody affair usually witnessed with great interest and excitement by the children. First the tension, as the slaughterman stalked the pig with a wire noose on the end of a pole trying to hook it over the animal's snout. Then a cheer as he succeeded, pulling the noose tight and hoisting the squealing animal up on to the rack where it hung, throat exposed and hind legs just clear of the ground. A bucket was placed underneath, the throat of the animal was slit and it was left to bleed to death. After the carcase had been put into the scalding tub it was cleaned and cut up into agreed portions for the families to share. Nothing was wasted, not even the bladder, which was blown up and given to the boys to play football with. Two-thirds of the meat eaten by farm labourers' families at this time was salted pork.

Meanwhile work in the harvest fields continued until sunset. When the labourer arrived home he ate, and then went straight to bed. After the harvesters came the gleaners, well-organised groups of old men, women and children who between them could collect sufficient wheat to supply each family in their syndicate with several bushels of flour for the winter months. Those months were often hard. Working hours were shorter and wages went down correspondingly to as low as 9s. od. a week. So the labourers who could get jobs as 'barntaskers', threshing the corn with flails in the warmth of one of the big barns, considered themselves lucky. Many men chose to increase the family income by putting their boys to work at the age of 9 or 10 years; they hired them out to farmers as horsekeepers or ploughboys for a year at 3s. 6d. a week, receiving an additional payment of £2 at the end of the year. The boys stayed at the farm throughout the week, sleeping in the mess room.

On Sundays they were allowed home, for that was the one day of the week when the family was together. They went to church or chapel and, although many of the adults could not read properly, they were not at a loss because they knew the entire service and most of the hymns and psalms by heart. Their pleasures were few and simple—going for walks, listening to the village band, taking part in the annual sports and, on rare occasions, marvelling at magic lantern slide lectures given by a visiting missionary, about faraway lands.

The most important event—as important as Christmas

or Easter—was Harvest Home, the day the last cartload of wheat or barley sheaves was brought from the fields to the big barn. The day of thanksgiving for the assurance of survival during the colder months ahead. Everyone turned out to see Harvest Home; the horse that pulled the final load of sheaves was gaily decorated with ribbon, brasses and hedgerow greenery and was followed to the barn by almost the entire community. Inside, the area where the threshing would later begin was temporarily cleared and laid out with benches and long trestle tables, each filled with huge joints of meat, dishes of vegetables and jugs of foaming ale. At the top table sat the farmer, his senior staff and their families; below them the craftsmen who did work for the estate—the wheelwright, the village saddler and the blacksmith. The parson was there, the servants and all the labourers and their families. A huge gathering that ate, drank, smoked and sang its way well into the night. Never a Harvest Home went by without a full-throated tribute to old John Barleycorn.

A pictorial record of the end of hay-making on a farm at Offley, near Hitchin, during the 1890s—probably taken to show the farmer's new elevator, which enabled him to build much bigger ricks.

'Then here's to Barley Mow, brave lads,
We'll drink to Barley Mow.'

And that they did—over and over again.

3

THE SMALL BUSINESS—
THE PERFUMERY

In 1823 Mr Edward Perks of Hitchin, a chemist and purveyor of hardware, embarked upon an expensive and uncertain commercial experiment which, if weather and soil conditions had been against him, could easily have ended in failure. As it was, the experiment succeeded; Mr Perks and his wife Sarah brought to Hertfordshire a small and colourful industry which was to earn their family a series of international awards and turn the town, during the summer months, into a Victorian tourist attraction.

'I will never erase from my mind,' enthused one such visitor, 'the impression made by coming suddenly upon a great expanse clothed with lavender in full blossom, the plants set in serrated ranks, cultivated to the extreme height of floral productiveness, and with no other tint to break the broad, level rich blue-grey blaze. The sight is striking indeed when the lights and shadows of a day of mingled sunshine and cloud flit over the fields, and deliver it most completely, by the wonderful effects of varying intensity of hue so occasioned, from any possible charge of sameness.'

Mr Perks, of course, was concerned not so much with stunning the visitors as with making a profit, and he had undoubtedly taken into account the financial risks involved. Although lavender has been cultivated in England since Elizabethan times it is not an indigenous plant. Having been introduced from Southern Europe, it is sensitive to the extremes of the English weather, and is a capricious plant that will only grow well on warm southerly-facing slopes and in a loamy soil which has been carefully prepared. However, Edward Perks' experiment was such a success, that by the 1840s when his son Samuel succeeded to the business, the family was cultivating thirty-five acres of land on slopes to the north and west of the town which yielded sufficient essential oil of lavender to produce well over two thousand gallons of fashionable lavender water annually. The acreage was not large, even for those days. At Mitcham, in Surrey, three hundred and fifty acres were being devoted to lavender cultivation, and yet this tiny independent industry was run successfully by three separate families for almost one hundred and fifty years.

The work cycle adopted by Sam Perks usually began around the first week in November, with a huge bonfire on which he and his men burned all the fifth-year plants which had begun to run to wood and were past service. 'This sacrifice,' wrote the Victorian visitor, 'is an annual thing and, so big are the bonfires and so powerful the aromatic fragrance given thus to the winds, that Hitchin to its last court and alley is for days together a town of sweet smells.' With the sacrifice over, the task of ploughing and preparing the ground for the following year's crop began, with a labourer employed at 12s. od. a week spreading between thirty and forty tons of manure to each acre. The method of propagation was from cuttings which, having proved themselves at a year's growth, were divided into two at the root and set half a yard apart. From this, a year later, they were planted out for stock purposes and began to yield. At this point, every other plant was removed and replanted elsewhere, thus leaving each young lavender bush a yard apart, with nine thousand of them to every acre.

The cropping, or harvesting, began when the plants were in their second year, although a plant was not considered to be at its best until the third summer. The harvests went well for Sam Perks until the year 1860 when, after a severe frost killed off most of his young plants, further calamity was caused by the arrival of a completely unknown disease which attacked the mature bushes just as they were beginning to flower and caused most of them to wither away. It began in the Surrey fields and spread, during the following years, with such devastation that the losses suffered by growers were enormous. One grower in Lincolnshire had to go out of business. The blight became known as *shab* and has affected crops to a lesser degree ever since. At the time of its first appearance the cause was attributed to over-manuring the land, thereby forcing the plants too much and rendering them more susceptible to disease. Sam Perks found the most effective way to remove it was to transplant his bushes in fresh soil.

Perks' Hitchin Lavender not only survived the blight, but also produced an essential oil of a quality which won international awards at the London Exhibition in 1862, and the Paris Exhibition in 1867. Nine years later, at the American Centennial Exhibition at Philadelphia, Samuel Perks 'Lavender Farmer and Chemist, of Hitchin, England' received a most coveted trophy, a medal, a diploma and a report for the outstanding quality of the essential oil of lavender. In a trade leaflet which he produced for that exhibition he described some of the problems of his industry:

'The cultivation of lavender is very expensive if well carried out,' he wrote. 'It is an uncertain crop, the yield of essential oil varying considerably, some seasons as much as 40 or 50 per cent less than others; it also depends much upon the weather during the months of May, June and July being bright and sunny, in which case a good yield is generally the result, but if wet weather sets in or an absence of sun, the quality is greatly reduced. An acre of lavender produces from three to six Winchester quarts, or 15 to 30 pounds weight, according to the season or age of the plants.'

The harvest, too, varied with the weather, usually beginning in the first week of August when, for 6d. a day and free lemonade, cottage women armed with small sickles spent long days cropping the bushes and binding the stalks of lavender into sheaves weighing just over 20 lbs. each. These were then carted down the hill to Sam Perks' small distillery at the back of his chemist's shop in the High Street, where they were prepared for the still. The women and children employed in the preparation sat in groups in the cobbled courtyard cutting off as much of the stalk as possible so as to ensure that only the finest bouquet of oil, from the blooms themselves, was obtained.

It was at this stage that the workers were confronted with the nastiest aspect of the job, the stings of drunken bees. As Sam Perks himself wrote: 'Their behaviour in lavender fields, especially towards the end of the season when the flowers are fully developed, cannot be too severely reprobated. . . . They refuse to leave their luscious feast even when it is laid on the trimming bench and hundreds of them are thrown into the still, notwithstand-

A regular summer sight behind the shop of Messrs Perks and Llewellyn during the 1880s. Women and children are busy cutting the lavender blooms from their stalks in preparation for the still—a task made somewhat hazardous by the hundreds of bees which clung stubbornly to the blooms in a state of intoxication.

46

ing the efforts to dislodge them, in a state of helpless intoxication.' If being boiled in the still wasn't very nice for the bees neither was the task performed by several small boys who were employed to climb into the still and tread down the lavender as it was loaded for distillation. They were inevitably severely stung and would have found little consolation from a comment which appeared in the *Pharmaceutical Journal* of 1877: 'After the first day or two the boys become so insensible to the poison that they feel but little pain when stung.'

Distillation of the lavender took several weeks and involved days of work that began at four o'clock in the morning and ended at ten o'clock at night. The blooms, having been packed into the still, were covered with water and sealed in. The still was then steam-heated until the steam inside carried the volatile oil of lavender over into the *worm*. This was a long coiled pipe which passed through a huge oak vat of cold water, causing the steam and oil in the pipe to condense and drip into the receiver waiting at the bottom. In his laboratory, Sam Perks filtered the oil to virtual purity; then the oil was left in uncorked bottles for three months so that it lost the strong 'still smell' before it was eventually corked and allowed to mature for three years. After that period it could either be retained as pure essential oil of lavender or diluted with spirit and other fragrant ingredients to become lavender water. Sam Perks, like every other manufacturing chemist, had his own secret formula for this preparation.

In Victorian times these products had a variety of medicinal and toiletry uses. Although it was no longer considered a cure for palsy, as the Elizabethans had believed, it was regarded as a method of relieving wind; two drops of pure lavender oil taken on a lump of sugar would do the trick. Lavender water, paradoxically, in view of the passion shown for the plant by bees, was an effective insect repellent. In country districts it was common practice to keep a lavender bush in the garden so that the

47

blossoms, steeped in vinegar, could be used to treat bruises. The ladies sprinkled Perks Lavender Water into their baths and over themselves, and hung little embroidered muslin bags of lavender bloom in their wardrobes to keep their clothes smelling sweet. The gentlemen dabbed lavender water on their faces and shaved with Perks Lavender Bloom Shaving and Toilet Soaps. There was also, before the advent of toothpaste, a Lavender Charcoal Dentifrice—a powder made from the flowers and wood of lavender; 'A new preparation,' wrote Mr Perks in 1876, 'that the proprietor believes has never before been introduced to the public.'

In 1876 Sam Perks took into partnership his manager C. W. H. Llewellyn to form the business of Perks and Llewellyn, by which name the company became best known. The two chemists did not always have an easy time promoting their products which were, after all, subject to the whims of fashion. They had to compete with the arrival from the continent of Eau de Cologne which,

Perks and Llewellyn's shop in 1897, decorated to celebrate the diamond jubilee of Queen Victoria.

48

they stoutly declared, was 'questionable in the long run to the simple fragrance of our good old English lavender'.

In 1907, by which time the business of Perks and Llewellyn had been acquired by a Richard Lewis, the suffragette Sylvia Pankhurst came to Hitchin on a fashion assignment for the *London Evening News*. 'Lavender water is falling on evil days,' she declared. 'People nowadays prefer more modern perfumes with strange sounding names. Hitchin is now the largest growing centre but even here a decreasing number of casual workers, both men and women, are employed. The women mostly are of the very poorest and the wages are very low.'

Her words had a ring of truth about them. Lavender oils and water were no longer in such great demand from the general public, and yet they were to remain sufficiently popular to justify the continuation of this little family business for a further generation. It was not until well into the second half of the 20th century that Perks and Llewellyn closed down and the final proprietor, Miss Violet Lewis, reluctantly allowed the last blue-grey field of lavender to be turned over to the less fragrant, but more nourishing, common cabbage.

4

THE LIFE OF THE POOR

Less than two hundred yards from Perks and Llewellyn's sweet-smelling lavender emporium, through the churchyard past St Mary's Church and across the River Hiz, there once stood Hitchin's least-prestigious contribution to the Victorian and Edwardian social scene. For most other residents of the town, the Queen Street slums were, to use the modern idiom, a no-go area; two or three acres of land on which huddled hundreds of crumbling cottages. Into these were crammed the poor, the inadequate, the criminal, and all others to whom that notable Victorian euphemism 'the rougher element' was normally applied. It was a district where policemen always patrolled in pairs and into which nobody who was not a resident liked to venture after dark. A small sore, admittedly, compared with the vast slum malignancies of the industrial cities, but one which was evident in every small town and which contributed to the Victorian housing scandal.

It is true that politicians had begun to tackle the problem of poor housing as early as the 1850s, with the passing of the first Public Health Acts, but it was not until 1875 that housing legislation was put on to a really sound foundation with the first laws which obliged slum landlords to either repair their properties or to demolish them, or face compulsory purchase orders from the local authorities. Even so, improvements were far from immediate and it was to be another fifty years before slum neighbourhoods such as the one in Hitchin began to disappear for good.

The Queen Street slums were made up of dozens of little cobbled courtyards leading off the main street every few yards: Chapman's Yard, Gascoigne's Yard, Webb's

Yard, Thorpe's Yard, Peahen Yard, Barnard's Yard. Each had a couple of dozen tiny cottages, the same one-up-one-down hovels as those inhabited by the farm workers but packed far more tightly together and with no gardens. Some had earth floors and each group of twenty-four families had to share a single cold water tap which stood in the centre of the yard. Also shared were the one or two earth closets tucked away in a corner. These were the people for whom Victorian social reformers were fighting in what was known as *the battle of the pig and sty*, acknowledging, in other words, that if Society insisted that some of its people should live in homes little better than pig-sties, then Society should not be surprised if they started behaving like swine.

In fact, many good families lived there, who though poor, were hard-working. The men laboured on the railway or at the local tannery, the women did seasonal work such as straw-plaiting or picking dandelions and other suitable wild plants which could be sold to William Ransome's

Queen Street slums, early 1900s.

distillery. Inevitably it was a very tough area; there were thirteen public houses, which along with the inhuman and overcrowded living conditions did much to provoke drunkenness, fighting and domestic disputes.

In the autumn of 1904, the owner of a block of these cottages in Barnard's Yard applied to the Hitchin Justices for eviction orders against a number of families upon whom he had served notices to quit, but who had refused to go. The case attracted little interest, the local newspaper reporting only briefly that the landlord wished to renovate the property and that the tenants (whom they did not bother to name) had been unable to find alternative accommodation. Their plea was borne out by Police Superintendent John Reynolds, who told the Court that, as far as he knew, there were no other cottages to let in the town. The justices granted the eviction orders, suspending them for a further four weeks so that the families might have more time to find other homes, but on the day the orders were served, 5th October, 1904, they were still there, and the police and bailiffs had to evict them forcibly. A brief but revealing account of the event appeared in the *Hertfordshire Express* the following Saturday:

'Some unusual scenes were witnessed in Queen Street on Wednesday when, under ejectment orders issued a month ago, Superintendant Reynolds and a number of constables removed the goods and chattels of a number of cottagers living in Barnard's Yard. For years the yard has been a cause of much difficulty owing to its insanitary state and the conditions under which the occupants have to live. Soon after ten o'clock the work began to the accompaniment of profuse anathemas hurled at the police, who had a very disagreeable task. Other things than furniture were found in the houses and as, in addition, some of the occupiers had been keeping poultry, pigeons and even a horse indoors, conditions were not of the most salubrious. The property was speedily removed and the erstwhile tenants had to survey their household goods in the open air. But neighbouring barns were quickly at their disposal and cover was found. A photographer (Mr H. G. Moulden) wishing to depict the scene had a rough time and had to be protected by the police as he went about his work. The important question left was how to deal with the eight people thus left homeless, and with the usual generosity of their class the neighbours solved it by taking in the outcasts.'

The last point illustrates one of the main reasons why, despite earlier legislation, the slum situation got worse in some places before it got better. It was all very well to demolish or restore decaying property, but those who lost their homes because of it were too poor to afford anything better, so the only course open to them was to seek refuge in other slums, which simply increased overcrowding and worsened living conditions elsewhere. The Great War made the situation worse by putting a virtual stop to all public and private building and in 1917, when the

The eviction in Barnard's Yard, 1904. It would seem that neither the police, the bailiff, the tenants nor the sight-seers could resist the temptation to pose for a formal photograph, despite the abuse which was hurled at the Law during the episode.

problem had reached crisis point, a Royal Commission blamed the appalling conditions of working class homes, not only for the industrial unrest but also for the alarming state of health of the poorer children. Of nearly two and a half million school children medically examined, nearly half were physically defective. Only after the signing of the Armistice did Parliament and people unite in a common pledge to build homes 'fit for heroes to live in'. Important reforms followed quickly which, while not without their imperfections, enabled local authorities to go ahead with schemes for estates of council houses, the Government covering the additional costs caused by higher wages and prices.

The Queen Street slums disappeared for good in the 1920s, their remains buried beneath the new town square which was named St Mary's Square after the church which it overlooks. The town council left an inscription on the steps which lead up to it from the River Hiz:

Corner of one of the many slum 'yards' off Queen Street, Hitchin, at the turn of the century.

'On the adjacent area formerly stood 174 cottages, which

were demolished under slum clearance schemes and the
occupants, 637 in number, housed elsewhere.
A.D. 1925–29.'

This was a considerable social achievement for a town the
size of Hitchin. For the majority of poor, life was a long
tragedy, and as the following history indicates, for many,
domestic service was the only future.

Alice was only 5 years old when they came to take her
away from her family. It was a painful moment and she
cried a lot, but the report of the inspector emphasised
the urgency of the situation. 'The family lives in the very
worst conditions in a slum cottage in Clerkenwell and the
widowed mother contacted our representative in a state
of great distress. She works as a cook and her wages are
such that she is quite unable to support her five children.
Consumption is a bad heritage. The father died from it,
the oldest son and a daughter are smitten with it. The
little girl, however, may be saved and probably will with
six or seven years of country life and air.'

So, on a summer afternoon in 1908, a kindly lady from
the Society calling itself The National Refuges for Homeless and Destitute Children, took Alice away from
London and her sick family and brought her to Hertfordshire. The little girl was one of a number whose destinies
were changed that summer, for Alice had become one of
the first children to go to a new home which the Society
had opened at Royston, as the first of its kind to cater
specifically for little girls between the ages of 5 and 10.
It was another step forward by the organisation founded
originally in 1843 to open *ragged schools* for destitute
children in the City of London, which was later amalga-
mated with the Earl of Shaftesbury's Arethusa Training
Ship Scheme for homeless boys to become the
Shaftesbury Homes and Arethusa.

At the turn of the century, the National Refuges for
Homeless and Destitute Children had more than a

55

thousand boys and girls in its care and yet was worried by the fact that it consistently had to refuse small girls like Alice because there was nowhere suitable for them to live. For this reason the Society bought a five-acre site on a chalk ridge overlooking Royston and built *The Home for Little Girls*. It was a combined home and school for eighty youngsters and run by a staff of three, a matron and two teachers, who between them commanded salaries which totalled just under £350 a year. The youngsters taken to the home that summer were victims, not simply of poverty, but of disease, malnutrition and ill-treatment. The health risks involved in bringing so many of them together under one roof so suddenly were considerable and, consequently, initial medical precautions taken by the matron were drastic. The head of each little girl was shaved and the hair burnt, and those found to be infected with lice were treated daily in baths of disinfectant, and for a short period of time each child had a weekly medical examination by a local doctor.

It was all to good effect, since a few weeks later in his

First occupants of the new Home for Little Girls, at Royston, in 1908, some with their heads still showing evidence of the shaving they received, as a precaution against lice. Somewhere among them is the little girl Alice whose case is briefly reported in this story.

139. ROYSTON THE HOME FOR LITTLE GIRLS

first report on the school, the local inspector, Mr Wix, found: 'The children are very orderly and delightfully happy and natural. Both divisions are taught with much thought and care and the school has made a promising start in excellent and well-equipped premises, where the children are under the influence of a good school and a happy well-ordered home.' Alice remained at Royston for five years until she was old enough to be transferred to the society's home at Ealing where, from the age of 10, she began to receive the training and discipline considered necessary to prepare for the only respectable and secure station in life then available for a girl in her position— domestic service. The training was described by the matron of the Ealing home in her report to the governors in the year that Alice reached her fifteenth birthday.

'So much has to be done in the way of mental health and moral instruction that it is manifest that a complete training in household work is impossible; but, as far as our means allow, the committee do the best that is possible. All the work at the home is done by the girls— sweeping, scrubbing, washing, dormitory work, cooking and sewing, and as each girl's period of residence is drawing to a close at the age of 15 they are subjected to special training fitting them for housemaid's work, some for the kitchen or the scullery according to their capabilities and leanings. Out of 40 girls discharged during the year 33 went into service, so that subscribers may feel assured that the training which has been given is really of value to the girls.'

The following year, when she was approaching her seventeenth birthday, Alice wrote a letter to her old matron on notepaper bearing a fashionable address in Hampstead, London.

'Dear Matron,
    I hope you are quite well and all the teachers. I know you will be pleased to hear that I am still getting on. I

57

had my second rise, making me £14 a year. I hope the measles at the school has quite gone by now, they always were such a worry to you. All being well I shall come to Old Girls' Reunion next Thursday week. It seems such a long time since I was at the dear old place. I sometimes wish I could come back again.

I remain, dearest matron, one of your Old Girls,

Alice.'

5

THE COMING OF THE MOTOR CAR

For the hundreds of people who witnessed it, the scene in Fore Street, Hertford, one Thursday afternoon in May 1903 was unforgettable. The air throbbed with noise and was filled with exhaust fumes as the county town experienced its first traffic jam. The pioneer motorists were there at the invitation of the town mayor in what was a calculated public relations exercise to help apprehensive country folk understand and accept the generally unwelcome advent of the motor car.

'We were all outlaws . . .' Pioneer motorist Kenneth Murchison at the tiller of his de Dion-Bouton Voiturette in 1901.

The motoring mayor of Hertford, Mr Kenneth Murchison, had become one of the county's first car-owners two years earlier, when he paid three hundred guineas for a $4\frac{1}{2}$ horse-power de Dion-Bouton Voiturette.

Many years later, as Sir Kenneth Murchison, High Sheriff of Northamptonshire, he was to recall: 'It is quite impossible now for people to have any real conception of the experiences, prejudices, hardships and insults which were suffered by the pioneers of motoring in this country.... We were all outlaws together and we felt that the police and public opinion were against us. If there was an accident anywhere it must have been our fault, even if we were not there and knew nothing of it.'

In the year of 1901, shortly after acquiring his de Dion, Sir Kenneth was among the handful of Hertfordshire car owners who each received a peremptory circular from the Chief Constable of the county, Colonel Henry Daniell:

'The Chief Constable desires to inform owners and drivers of Motor Vehicles in the County of Hertford that constant complaints are made to him of the alarm and danger to the public caused by the reckless driving of some of these vehicles.

'The Chief Constable reminds owners and drivers that the speed at which a motor car may be driven on a highway is limited by law to TWELVE MILES AN HOUR. It by no means follows that this speed may be sustained when Motor Cars are passing or meeting other vehicles or horses, or when passing through towns, villages or other inhabited places. On each of these occasions it is incumbent on the drivers of Motor Cars to reduce their speed to such a pace as would be safe and reasonable were the vehicles drawn by horse instead of mechanical power. Failure to observe this precaution will render the driver of the Motor Car liable to prosecution under Article IV., Sec. I., of the Locomotives on Highways Act, 1896....'

The circular illustrates perfectly the fierce opposition which the early motorists met from a rural population still firmly convinced that the horse was the only respectable and reliable form of road transport. Unfortunately, it was the horses which were caused most distress by the presence of a car upon the road. Even when driven slowly, the noise of the engine and the dust it created were sufficient to make the most passive beast restive; the more volatile ones frequently became so terrified that they bolted, often throwing and injuring the rider.

Recalling from his diary the first time he took his wife for a ride in the de Dion, Sir Kenneth wrote: 'She sat in the front seat facing the way we were going, with nothing whatever between her feet resting on a board which folded forward for the purpose, and anything we might run into. We did run into several things that day —mostly animals, because we met a lot of beasts going to the Annual County Agricultural Show.'

As it happened, the critics of the motor car had a champion in the Chief Constable, for Colonel Daniell was a dedicated horseman. At one time, he even considered bicycles to be dangerous. When some of his constables were issued with the machines in 1896 to catch *scorchers* (speeding cyclists) on the Great North Road, he decided that the operation was sufficiently dangerous to justify awarding his men an extra 3d. an hour danger money! Little wonder, then, that the colonel, while a very fair-minded man, set out to offer the horse-owning majority as much protection from the motor car as the Law allowed.

Although in his first two years of motoring Sir Kenneth received his fair share of personal abuse from the public, it was an incident which occurred in a main street in Hertford which almost certainly drove home the need for a publicity campaign to help the public not only accept the motor car, but also to realise that it was here to stay. He was driving his de Dion at a sedate 8 miles an hour when an elderly woman started to cross the road about ten yards ahead of him. When she saw the car coming she let out a wail, clasped her hands together and fell face downwards to the ground. There she remained motionless, apparently resigned to the fate of being crushed to death by the monster that was bearing down upon her. In fact, Sir Kenneth stopped easily several feet short of the 'body', which remained motionless for several more moments before the old lady finally rose, dazed and quite unable to believe that she was still alive.

So, in conjunction with the Automobile Club, the Mayor of Hertford set about arranging an Automobile Demonstration on the streets of the county town, which, he hoped would prove 'how slowly motors could go, and how quickly they could stop'. The week before the demonstration, the *Hertfordshire Mercury* carried a letter from the Mayor to warn the public of the event, 'in order that those whose horses are afraid of motor cars may know that there will be, if fine, a good many cars in and about the town that day. Also, that there may be a good many people who would like to avail themselves of this opportunity to accustom their horses to motors, standing still or in motion.'

Sir Kenneth also invited the Chief Constable to lunch with him and other members of the Automobile Club before the demonstration, and to propose the toast 'The Progress and Welfare of Automobilism'. Colonel Daniell accepted gracefully and, during his speech, put forward the interesting idea that cars of motorists convicted of reckless driving should be made to carry some special identification 'which would be an indication that the driver was a suspected character and would cause his driving to be more closely supervised by the police'.

The demonstration, which attracted some thirty cars from all over the country, was a great success, not least the event which involved a series of comparative braking contests between a car and a horse-drawn vehicle. There were gasps of surprise from the crowd when, on every occasion and despite their higher speeds, the cars proved to have the more efficient brakes. When the time came for Sir Kenneth to demonstrate his own vehicle, he chose a steep hill leading down into the town and invited the wary Chief Constable to join him as a passenger.

'Just as we started,' Sir Kenneth recalled, 'he gripped the side of the car firmly and said "You be careful and remember I'm an old man". I remember going down the hill as quickly as I could—he looked as though we were going to shoot the rapids at Niagara. Having had my brakes smothered with French chalk I knew I could pull up in a very short distance: I must have been going between 25 and 28 miles an hour when the signal, a dropped handkerchief, was unexpectedly given half-way down the hill; a few yards sufficed in which to bring the de Dion to a standstill. The result was received with tumultuous applause by the watching crowd.'

In its journal the following month, the Automobile Club reported: 'That Hertfordshire will prove a paradise for motor cars is certain so long as drivers pay due consideration to other users of the road, and only drive at

One of Britain's first motor rallies, held in Hertford in 1903.

63

higher speeds on perfectly open and unoccupied roads. The police are very reasonable and favourably disposed towards motorists, two of them even going so far as to assist one of the visitors who had the misfortune to puncture, with a repair to his tyres.'

Nevertheless, as we shall see, accidents could happen.

On 30th April, 1906, shortly before mid-day, a motor car crossed the border into Hertfordshire. It was a beautiful car, an 18 horse-power Peugeot, fashioned by French engineers and coach-builders with all the elegance of the Edwardian period. It had a mass of gleaming brass fittings and the coachwork of dark green and varnished wood was built in the Brougham style, making it reminiscent of the enclosed horse-drawn carriage which it was replacing. The upholstery was of buttoned leather, the windows of the enclosed rear compartment were fitted with dainty lace curtains and there was an electric light and a speaking tube, through which the occupants could issue instructions to their chauffeur. There was nobody in the rear compartment on this day; the sole passenger was sitting alongside the driver on the open front seat, protected only by a plate-glass windscreen.

Charles Preston, aged 52, 'a gentleman of Lancaster', was travelling south to London in a car owned by his cousin, and driven by her chauffeur, Albert Carter, aged 31, from Ashford. They had left Lancaster the day before, stopping overnight in Coventry before beginning the final stage of their journey down the old Watling Street to London. Carter, an experienced chauffeur, had driven some 75,000 miles during the three years in which he had held his licence. That day, he had been at the wheel for about two and a half hours as they passed through the village of Markyate and on towards St Albans.

At about the same time, a mile or so further south, two other men were beginning a more routine journey. Horace Pedder and his brother Alfred of Flamstead village, were making their way down Pepperstock Lane towards the London road, each in charge of a horse and cart. They were on their way to load up with animal fodder which they were due to cart to London later that day. At the junction of the lane with the main road, Horace was in front leading his horse on foot. He was half-way across the main road when he heard his brother shout, but it was too late.

The Peugeot hit them broadside on, pushing the heavy cart and stricken animal twenty yards up the road and throwing Horace Pedder on to the grass verge. The sight which confronted the rescuers was not pleasant. Horace Pedder was screaming with the pain from two broken legs. The horse, lying in a tangle of broken shafts and harness, was so badly injured it had to be destroyed. Albert Carter, the chauffeur, apparently protected to a degree by his leather-covered steering wheel, had only superficial injuries and was kneeling beside his passenger, who had been less fortunate. Charles Preston had been

The scene on 30th April, 1906 shortly after the collision between the car and the horse and cart. The horse lies dying and, behind the overturned wagon, a group stands watching a doctor tend Mr Charles Preston, the car passenger, who was to die in hospital later that night.

thrown forward violently by the impact of the collision; his face had been torn dreadfully by the glass of the windscreen and his jaw, nose and skull shattered on impact with the heavy wooden cart.

Within a short time a policeman, a doctor and a clergyman were on the scene. They put splints on the injured wagon man and carefully carried Charles Preston across to a nearby public house which, ironically, bore the name *The Waggon and Horses.* Preston, despite his terrible injuries, was conscious for some time and repeatedly asked the same question, 'Were we to blame?' It was a question which he never heard answered, for he died that night at the West Hertfordshire Infirmary. Meanwhile, for his distressed chauffeur there began an ordeal which lasted for three months, as machinery of the law was set into motion to try to find the answer to the question asked by his dying passenger.

There was no worse place in England for Albert Carter to have been involved in such an accident at such a time.

The 18 horse-power French Peugeot, with sightseers, after the crash. Such was the interest in the motor fatality that postcards printed by the photographer sold in their hundreds.

66

For Markyate villagers were still recovering from the death, a year earlier, of little Willie Clifton, aged 4, after he had been struck down in the High Street by a car which had failed to stop. It was the first hit-and-run fatality ever known in England and it had caused a national furore. So much so that Sir Alfred Harmsworth, proprietor of the *Daily Mail*, offered a reward of £100 for information leading to the discovery of the vehicle.

The money was never paid because of what the *Daily Mail* later referred to as 'one of the most amazing coincidences on record'; the owner of the elusive car turned out to be none other than Sir Alfred's brother, Mr Hildebrand Harmsworth! No member of the Harmsworth family was in the car at the time and it was only after Mr Harmsworth himself had read the story and initiated enquiries with Scotland Yard and the Hertfordshire Police that the full story emerged. Harmsworth's chauffeur, a Spaniard named Rocco Cornalbas, had been driving two of his employer's friends to London when the accident happened. Thinking he had caught the little boy 'only a light, glancing blow', Cornalbas decided he had probably not been hurt and had driven on. At least, that was his story when he stood trial for manslaughter at Hertfordshire Assizes in July 1905. He was found guilty and sentenced to six months' hard labour.

Now, less than a year later, a second chauffeur faced a similar charge. Albert Carter was accused of the manslaughter of his passenger. At his trial, as at the inquest on Charles Preston, the outcome hinged almost entirely upon estimates of the speed at which the Peugeot had been travelling immediately before the collision with the horse and cart. On this, there was considerable disagreement. Some claimed the Peugeot went through Markyate's High Street at between 20 and 30 miles an hour. The landlord of the *Green Man* said it went past his pub 'like a flash of lightning'. Others said the speed was much lower than that, and blamed the wagoner, Horace Pedder, for completely misjudging the speed of the car before leading his horse and cart out into the road.

Carter himself said he was travelling at between 15 and 18 miles an hour just prior to the crash and claimed he had been sounding his horn all the way along the road. However, under cross-examination, he agreed that—having travelled the 62 miles from Coventry to Markyate in just under two and a half hours—his average speed for the journey must have been at least 23 miles an hour. It was probably that admission which led the jury to reach a verdict of Guilty, with a strong recommendation for leniency in view of Carter's good record. That recommendation was reflected in the sentence of two months' imprisonment imposed on the chauffeur at Hertfordshire Assizes on 6th July, 1906.

The conclusion of that trial enabled Hertfordshire Police to close their file on what became known as The Markyate Motor Tragedies. Yet, while closing a file, they were in fact opening a whole new book. For this had been their first taste of a new and hideous event which was to be repeated as many as a hundred times a year upon the roads of Hertfordshire: Death by Motor Vehicle.

6

THE PARSON AND A RURAL LIVING

Even parsons have nightmares. A common one is experienced during difficult fund-raising campaigns when the good men, trying to find sufficient cash for urgent church repairs become susceptible to nocturnal visions of God's House falling down about them. The Reverend Ralph Lindsay Loughborough suffered such a vision in 1875. His church fell down and, unfortunately, it was not in a dream.

In 1851, when the population was flocking to London to see the marvels of Victorian achievement on display at the Prince Consort's great Crystal Palace Exhibition in Hyde Park, Mr Loughborough left the capital and brought his wife to a new and humble living in Hertfordshire —where many of the less wonderful aspects of Victorian life were still on display. He brought her to the village of Pirton, a far cry from their cosy living in South London, which demanded of them qualities approaching those of a missionary taking Christianity to a foreign land. Loughborough's problem was that he was the first resident vicar to be appointed to Pirton for more than two hundred years and during the whole of that time the village, with its large and impressive Norman church, had been incorporated with the neighbouring parish of Ickleford, three miles away. There, successive rectors, pre-occupied with their own affairs, had allowed Pirton and the church to become a neglected satellite where parishioners had to organise their own service as best they could and where Holy Communion was celebrated only three times a year by a curate who had to trudge across the fields from Ickleford.

The parson, who had even to build his own vicarage

The Rev. Ralph Loughborough, towards the end of his forty-year
ministry as first Vicar of Pirton, Hertfordshire.

before he could move to Pirton, soon discovered that the church of St Mary had crumbled away to a condition that invited disaster. The South Transept, which formed the right arm of the cruciform plan, had already collapsed, and the Vestry was a damp little wooden hut leaning against the wall of the tall tower which itself was showing some alarming cracks. The only repairs carried out had been of a make-shift character, the more ominous holes having been hastily filled with mortar and hidden with plaster and brickwork.

Ralph Loughborough tried to launch a fund-raising scheme among his parishioners but his efforts were futile. The plain fact was that they had no money. Of a population of 1,100, all but a handful were families with an average income of £1 a week, the men working as farm labourers, the women and children supplementing the family income by straw-plaiting. Neither was there a wealthy squire nor any other landowner living in the parish who might be persuaded to make a large contribution towards the restoration of St Mary's Church. Nevertheless, early in 1871, the vicar decided to call in an eminent London church architect, J. L. Pearson, to survey St Mary's and put forward estimates for the restoration. Pearson reported that the collapse of the South Transept earlier had weakened the tower, which would need to be strengthened before the transept could be rebuilt. He also discovered that the roof above the Nave was in a dangerous state and would have to be completely replaced; a project which would cost the then enormous sum of £2,000. In fact, the situation was to prove even worse than the experienced architect had predicted.

Since their own parishioners had no money, Ralph and Marianna Loughborough decided to direct their money-raising campaign towards the neighbouring towns and parishes in the diocese. Night after night they spent hours at their desks, writing personal letters and composing appeal leaflets and advertisements. At the end of a few weeks, there was hardly a bishop, a priest or businessman who was not aware of the appalling state of St Mary's Church. Loughborough didn't mince his words in these letters: 'There is no vestry, nor other convenience for the officiating minister,' he wrote. 'The font, prayer desk, pulpit and doors are of the commonest description and utterly unworthy of the House of God.' This spirited campaign inevitably attracted the attention of the Press; a correspondent of the *Hertfordshire Express* went to see things for himself and returned to pen indignantly: 'Time and the ignorance and barbarism of past generations have well-nigh done their worst to efface the comeliness of God's House. There are doors, windows, fittings and appliances that no man of ordinary respectability would think good enough to call his own.'

By this time the 'gentleman parson' had become more than a spiritual leader to the people of Pirton. The tall man, with his fierce beard and forceful personality, epitomised the sort of man who dominated life in most other villages at that time. So the village boys bowed and the little girls curtsied when Mr Loughborough and his lady went past and the elder ones christened him 'The Squire'. The local Baptists, on the other hand, treated him with rather less respect, having become firmly established during the years in which St Mary's had no resident parson. They took great exception to his bombastic pulpit-thumping and their lay-preachers frequently waylaid him and attempted to 'expose his wrong teaching'. The bigotry and religious intolerance displayed by both sides resulted in many fierce arguments, Loughborough throwing eloquent bible quotations in support of his beliefs, only to find himself ducking a return volley of fresh ones that put the Baptist case equally effectively. According to the Baptists the Vicar, at this point, was obliged to cover his retreat by resorting to quotations from the 'unknown languages' of Greek and Latin of

Scene at St. Mary's Church, Pirton, in July 1876, a year after the church tower collapsed. The vicar, the Rev. Ralph Loughborough, is the taller figure with the beard in the centre of the photograph.

which, conveniently, he was the village's only exponent.

Nevertheless, he commanded tremendous respect from his own flock and when the time came in 1875 to begin the repair work on the church, there was no shortage of volunteers; the poor came forward and offered their time and energy in lieu of money. The team that began the repair work had been warned that the sixty feet tower of St Mary's was unsafe, so it was with some caution that they began to peck at the area around the base, intending to replace the crumbling stone with fresh blocks of clunch-stone quarried from the local pit. Hardly had the first pick-axe been driven in when the workmen became aware of movement. Then, in the words of a witness, 'the whole lower portion of the tower came away, rushing down like a stream of water'. By the grace of God, presumably, the top section of the tower was made of stronger material, having apparently been re-built two or three hundred years after the original base and so, incredibly, it did not fall but remained there suspended

73

precariously between the upper walls and roof of the Nave and Chancel.

The disaster meant, of course, a complete revision of plans. Far from damaging morale, the incident served to strengthen the determination of those involved. The top of the tower was quickly demolished and plans for the construction of the South Transept were abandoned so that all effort could be concentrated on rebuilding the huge tower. Tons more fresh clunch-stone had to be quarried while the masons salvaged as much as they could from the ruins of the old tower.

In July 1876, a dozen clergymen and other guests from the neighbouring parishes which had supported the appeal gathered with the villagers and workmen for a service to commemorate the laying of the corner-stone to the new tower. It seems difficult to believe that just six months later, on a frosty January Sunday, the tower was restored and re-opened to a joyous peal of bells, a sound which had not been heard in Pirton for very many years.

Meanwhile the campaign for money—which had already been running for six years—was resumed with renewed vigour. Loughborough's wife, Marianna, achieved a most remarkable coups with an imaginative advertisement placed in the columns of *The Times* newspaper.

T WENTY THOUSAND SHILLINGS—Who will help? A clergyman's wife WANTS to raise the SUM to assist in the reparation of a large church in the midst of a poor rural community. Tower so unsafe had to be taken down; rest of building much decayed. Please send one shilling to Mrs Loughborough, Pirton Vicarage, near Hitchin.

The response was remarkable. From the length and breadth of England, and from Scotland, too, the shillings cascaded in. Hundreds of them, each to be recorded meticulously by the Vicar in his Restoration Fund accounts book. In the end, the couple raised more than £3,000, which was sufficient to repair the church and re-furnish the interior. Ralph Loughborough died in 1895 at the age of 76, and Marianna twelve years later. After her funeral, the new vicar and the wardens of this now thriving parish church had little difficulty in deciding upon a memorial. They would build the South Transept which Ralph Loughborough had planned but had been forced to abandon because of the collapse of the tower.

Once again the volunteers came forward—seventy men and boys from the village—who, over a period of six years, quarried sufficient clunch-stone to build the transept. The walls, three feet thick, required one hundred and fifty cart-loads of material. Much of the work, the masonry, the carpentry, the plumbing and the carting, was done free of charge. The wives raised money for a tracery window, the children collected for the new oak door. The transept was completed and opened as a vestry in 1913:

St. Mary's Church, Pirton, after the restoration work.

'A memorial to Ralph Lindsay Loughborough, first sole Vicar of Pirton, and his wife Marianna. Two servants of God who laboured in Pirton for nearly half a century and who were lovingly enshrined in the hearts of those they left behind.'

7

THE POACHERS

Only Charles Dickens would have dared to invent such a pair—a brace of poachers, twin brothers, who shared the name of Fox! Yet, as gamekeepers, policemen and magistrates in North Hertfordshire came to learn, these characters were very much alive; a couple of likeable villains who between them managed to notch up two hundred convictions and whose nocturnal activities made them a legend in their own lifetime. They even earned themselves a modest space on the wall of Scotland Yard's Black Museum where, billed as *The Most Infamous Poachers of All Time*, they offer a modicum of light relief to an otherwise grisly show.

The Fox twins were born in the autumn of 1857 to Henry and Charlotte Fox, of Ten Acre Farm, Symond's Green, near Stevenage. Henry was reputedly descended from George Fox, the founder of the Quaker Society of Friends, and was a deeply religious man who had earned a good reputation as a preacher. He was also a regular worshipper at the Ebenezer Strict Baptist Chapel in Albert Street, Stevenage, which presumably prompted him in a moment of devout loyalty to christen his boys Ebenezer Albert and Albert Ebenezer. As it was, by giving his identical sons almost identical names, their father innocently helped them to escape almost as many charges as they were convicted on.

Albert and Ebenezer began to learn about and love the country almost as soon as they could walk; their lusting after its forbidden fruits emerged not long afterwards. By the time they were 10 they knew every copse and meadow for miles around their little farmstead. At the age of 11, they left school and were found jobs on neighbouring

THE FOX TWINS

Original 'mug shots' of the Fox Twins from police records show how the Law was eventually able to distinguish one twin from the other without going through the laborious Bertillon system of measuring height, head, hands and feet. Prints taken of the right ring fingers of the twins are completely different.

farms but they didn't like them. The same year, they set a gin-trap and caught their first rabbit. In 1871, at the age of 14, they were caught by a gamekeeper, poaching on his estate with a stolen gun. Henry Fox did the best he could for his sons; he engaged a solicitor who pleaded that the two innocent lads were only indulging in an isolated, if misguided, prank and should never have been prosecuted. The magistrate on the Hitchin bench agreed and the boys were let off. A month later, the same gamekeeper caught them again and they appeared before the same magistrate on the same charge—this time without a solicitor. A 10s. od. fine was recorded, the first of a list of poaching convictions that ended nearly seventy years later when the last of the twin Foxes was called to earth.

During that period Ebenezer collected eighty-two convictions and Albert one hundred and eighteen; the difference accounted for by the fact that Albert survived his brother by nearly twelve years. The twins also lost vast amounts of equipment, confiscated by the courts; more than fifty guns, ranging from flint-locks to muzzle and breech-loaders, hundreds of snares and traps, scores of yards of silk netting (to trap pheasant and partridge) and around five hundred yards of string netting (for rabbits). They always worked with a lurcher, a cross between a greyhound and a sheepdog, the combined characteristics of which made it ideal for poaching. Working with a lurcher, they once netted a thousand rabbits in one month. At night, they worked with the foresights of their guns either covered with white chalk or tipped with the head of a lucifer match which gave a small luminous glow when dampened. Albert, who emerged the stronger and better-natured of the twins, was also the better shot. He once bagged eight pheasants with one barrel but, at the same time, could kill cleanly when he wanted, bringing down a bird with just one or two pellets from the extreme edge of his spread of grapeshot.

Inevitably, with each succeeding court case, the twins' poaching reputation was further enhanced. Magistrates were often held spellbound, not only by the evidence of the police and gamekeepers but also by the highly imaginative defence pleas submitted by the defendants. Each time they appeared before the bench they maintained a well-practised attitude of hurt innocence. They were short stout men, just five feet two inches high with gnome-like figures and puckish faces of weather-beaten mahogany brown to match. Ebenezer, caught once in Hitch Wood, Preston, at dead of night, after first managing successfully to hide his gun and his bag, was nevertheless brought before the Hitchin bench the following Tuesday. 'All right Fox,' said the Chairman. 'I acknowledge you were without game or gun when arrested. But can you tell me why you were there, in a wood at dead of night, if not for an illegal purpose?'

'The truth was sir', replied Ebenezer, 'I was there to meditate upon the Baptist hymn book.' While the court

The twins outside a pub in Stevenage—Albert with their lurcher dog, Ebenezer nursing his 12-bore.

clutched its sides for several minutes, Ebenezer, displaying some annoyance at the hilarity, delved angrily into the deep pocket of his black poaching coat. After rummaging around for several minutes he finally held aloft in triumph, amid a small cloud of feathers, the Baptist hymn book which his father had given him as a boy.

The twins' only really successful defence was that of mistaken identity. After a while, they took to poaching singly and, when caught, each gave the other's name instead of his own. The keepers, unable to tell one from the other, had to accept what they were given. Thus, when Albert appeared in court charged under his brother's name, he could ask for, and frequently got, a dismissal on the grounds of a technicality. Many times a policeman or a keeper hesitated in the box under cross-examination when asked by one of the twins whether he was absolutely sure it was the defendant and not his brother whom he had seen on a dark night.

Sometimes it worked, sometimes it didn't. When it didn't there was usually a fine of a guinea or two or, if the twins weren't very flush at the time, a fortnight in gaol at Bedford, Hertford or St Albans. Their 'mistaken identity' plea was scuttled for good in 1901 when the Metropolitan Police Commissioner, Sir Edward Henry, introduced finger-printing as a standard part of all criminal records. Within a year or two of the opening of Scotland Yard's finger-print department, the Home Counties followed suit and in 1904 the twins were among the first group of criminals in Britain to be convicted on corroborative evidence based on their finger-prints. Albert and Ebenezer accepted all this with good heart, as they did their fines and imprisonment. It was one reason why they became so popular; gamekeepers, policemen and magistrates all agreed, they were always courteous—two of the most courteous liars they had ever come across.

Their charm, no doubt, was the main reason why they developed a considerable rapport with the local landed gentry whose preserves in North and Mid-Hertfordshire they regularly poached. One lady of the manor, well aware of Albert's devastating nightly exploits into her game preserves, even resorted to offering him protection money, approaching him personally at the opening of the pheasant season with the promise of a sovereign a week and a brace of pheasant, provided he agreed to keep off her land. The proposition was too good to turn down; Albert accepted gracefully and kept his word—leaving brother Ebenezer to poach the good lady's land on his own that winter! It was the ever-resourceful Albert who, when fined £1 by the St Albans bench for poaching, respectfully asked for twenty-four hours in which to find the money. The request granted, he spent the night on the estate owned by the magistrate who had imposed the fine. Next morning he turned up at St Albans Market with several brace of pheasant which he disposed of in no time. He then marched round to the offices of the Justices' Clerk, paid his fine and set off back to Stevenage and home. Home for the twins, after their parents' farmhouse fell into decay through neglect, was a primitive gipsy-type hut which they built for themselves entirely from twigs, branches and turf. They called it *Woodbine Cottage.*

By the year 1915, when Albert chalked up his hundredth poaching conviction, the twins' career had reached a peak. They chose to celebrate it with a rare period of honest wage earning, working for several weeks as hod-and-mortar carriers for the men building a new and impressive edifice in the centre of Stevenage. It was an irony which the locals could scarcely ignore, for Albert and Ebenezer were helping to build the new police station and magistrates' court. So the *North Herts Mail*, only weeks after recording Albert's 'century', was moved to feature the twins again, picturing them this time at work on the cells which, in fact, they later became the first to occupy! It is perhaps an indication of the affection which these old rascals enjoyed that the newspapers did not stoop so low as to refer to them as poachers, but as 'those genial sporting gentlemen who are familiar figures in the local courts on Game Law summonses'.

The twins could also claim to have a Royal Seal of Approval, if not on their poarching activities, then certainly on their skill as shots. It was placed upon Albert by that other genial sporting gentleman, Edward, Prince of Wales (later King Edward VII), in the public bar of the *Marquis of Lorne* one summer lunchtime in 1900. The Prince was motoring to Newmarket races when his car broke down in Stevenage High Street and while the repairs were carried out, he spent half an hour in the pub, during which time Albert was introduced to him. Far from being overwhelmed by the occasion, Albert recognised a fellow sportsman and was soon swapping yarns with him. It is said that when the Prince's equerry returned to the pub to tell Edward that the repairs to his car were completed, the Prince introduced Albert to him

The poachers during a brief spell of honest work—Ebenezer (left) and Albert as hod-and-mortar carriers during the building of Stevenage Police Station, the cells of which they became the first to occupy.

as 'a man who can shoot more birds by moonlight than you have shot by day'.

It is not difficult to understand why they were so popular; the crime they chose to live by may once have been punishable by hanging, but it is also the crime which appeals most to the man frustrated by the trappings of civilisation. A comparatively harmless crime which demands of the perpetrator all the basic instincts and qualities of Man the Hunter; an absolute knowledge of the wild animal and its territory, stealth, cunning, courage, a sharp eye and a cool nerve. The Fox twins had all these qualities and so were quietly envied and admired.

It was a pity, then, that Ebenezer should have tarnished their sporting reputation by committing a vicious and uncharacteristic crime, by inflicting grievous bodily harm upon a gamekeeper who caught him at work during a night poaching exercise. It was always reckoned that Ebenezer was the weaker of the two, the one who panicked when they were on the run, and it was this panic that caused him to lash out when he found himself trapped. He paid dearly for the mistake, receiving a sentence of ten years' penal servitude from the judge at Hertfordshire Assizes.

When they finally let him out he was an old man. He tried a job or two and started going regularly to the Baptist Chapel from which he had received his name. He even tried poaching again but found he was too deaf to work efficiently any more. Eventually, in his late sixties, he could look after himself no more and was taken to the Hitchin Infirmary at the old Chalkdell Workhouse. In September 1926, he became aware that he was dying, and clearly made up his mind that he wasn't going to do that in the unaccustomed comfort of a hospital ward under the public gaze of attendant doctors and nurses. So, dressed in pyjamas of hospital blue, he stole out one night and made off towards his old hunting territory. He got through Hitchin and half-way towards his birthplace

84

at Symond's Green before his tired legs gave out. He managed to crawl into a woodland thicket and was found there three days later. At Ebenezer's inquest, the coroner recorded a verdict of death from exposure and exhaustion.

Albert went on poaching and lived to enjoy his 80th year before he, too, was taken to the infirmary to die. Many old friends and enemies turned up to see him buried near his brother in St Nicholas churchyard, Stevenage. Those who couldn't come sent wreaths—landowners he had robbed, a magistrate who had sent him down, Baptists who had prayed for him and poulterers who had been his receivers. All had their feelings adequately summed up by the verse that accompanied a wreath from the Hitchin lawyer and historian, Reginald Hine:

'Gone to earth old friend
And lost to mortal view.
Good luck to you where'er you wend
Fresh woods and pastures new.'

8

THE RIOT

For the loyal townspeople of Watford, as for everyone else in the British Empire, Thursday, 26th June, 1902, should have been a day of joy and celebration. It was, after all, more than sixty years since a monarch had been crowned in Westminster Abbey, and Watford like every other town and village, had been planning to mark the event with festivities on a scale never attempted before. In fact, neither event took place. On the day set aside for his coronation, King Edward VII was lying on a couch in Buckingham Palace fighting for his life and two hundred loyal citizens of Watford were fighting to protect their shops and homes from a rampaging mob of rioters who caused bloodshed and committed arson, looting, and widespread damage before they were finally quelled.

The nation had been given little warning of the Coronation crisis. Only forty-eight hours beforehand they had been stunned by the news from Buckingham Palace that King Edward had undergone a major operation for perityphlitis (appendicitis) and that the surgeons were concerned about his condition. The Coronation, of course, would have to be postponed. As it turned out the surgery performed by Sir Frederick Treves proved highly successful but since the operation was comparatively new and reckoned to carry a high degree of risk, the early bulletins on the condition of the 'illustrious patient' gave no cause for optimism. Thus, a week that had promised to be so full of good things turned into one of gloom and anxiety. The hundreds of little committees set up to organise local festivities met hurriedly to assess the situation and without exception set about cancelling their events.

Francis Fisher of Watford. Businessman, civic leader and prime target of the rioters.

At Watford the task fell upon Francis Fisher, a local butcher and businessman who was also Chairman of the Town Council. He called his Coronation Committee together and all agreed that they had no option but to postpone the festivities; the children's sports in Cassiobury Park, the dinner for the aged and poor, the band concerts and procession and the lighting of the giant bonfire. Neither would it be right at this stage to give each child in the town the Coronation shilling which had been promised. Not when at any moment the nation might be mourning a dead king.

The announcement of the postponement was accepted with great disappointment but without question by most citizens, and on Wednesday the flags and bunting and other elaborate street decorations were taken down. The bonfire was left, hopefully to be lit at a later, happier, date in the summer.

The Thursday on which the Coronation should have taken place was hot and sultry. Few people bothered to go to work and crowds wandered listlessly about the town discussing the latest bulletin on the king's health but still feeling a great sense of anticlimax. As the day stretched towards evening there became apparent a feeling of unease and tension as groups of 'the rougher element' began moving through the crowds voicing more concern about their lost pleasures than for the health of their king. As they began uttering vague demands for some form of compensation, others, sensing an outlet for their disappointment, joined in. It was not long before the name of the unfortunate Councillor Francis Fisher was mentioned.

So it was that at 9.30 p.m. the elderly watchman who sat in his wooden hut guarding the bonfire witnessed with alarm a crowd of between two and three hundred people descending upon him. The ringleaders told him that since Fisher wasn't going to light his bloody bonfire, they would do it for him, and if he dared to show up, he'd end up on top of it! The huge, tinder-dry fire was blazing in a matter of moments; the old watchman was punched and bundled out of his hut which was hurled on to the fire along with the temporary fencing and other council property in the area. The town surveyor, a Mr Waterhouse, arrived to try to damp down the situation but was promptly pelted with stones. He had to take refuge in a nearby cottage which had all its windows smashed, before the mob—armed with wooden clubs, lengths of metal piping and pockets full of stones—made off towards the town centre to 'do for Fisher'.

Being in the centre of a mob during the moments building up to a full-scale riot is an uncanny experience. An angry crowd generates a tension and atmosphere of such strength that one feels one can literally reach out and touch it. The leaders and more volatile individuals move restlessly about, eyes searching for a movement, ears listening for a remark that will give them their first excuse to trigger off the violence. Such was the atmosphere in Watford High Street late that Thursday night. It was the movement of a solitary arm that set the violence under way. A stone flew through the air and the sound of breaking glass echoed down the street. A moment of silence . . . then, as if given a signal, the whole crowd surged forward to commit that offence which (short of treason) is the gravest form of a breach of the peace known to the English law—a riot.

The situation was one which the chief of Watford's Police Force, Superintendent Wood, was quite unable to control. Even with his full complement of some twenty men he would never have been able to contain the riot; not long before the incident began to build up, he had had to despatch half his force to Hemel Hempstead to deal with a series of minor disturbances there. So he was left with an inspector, a sergeant and a handful of mounted and foot-patrol constables. As Wood frantically telephoned neighbouring forces for more men, the mob proceeded to wreak its fury on Councillor Fisher's butcher's shop and on three other buildings, two drapery stores and a shoe shop which belonged to another member of the misunderstood Coronation Committee, Mr George Longley.

Francis Fisher had received some warning of the trouble and, with some of his staff, was attempting to barricade his premises when the rioters arrived. Although having little chance against the wall of flailing staves and metal piping they put up a stout defence for a short while, at one time slamming down the metal window shutters on the hands of several of the leading rioters who had smashed the windows and were trying to climb into the shop. The action sparked off a sensational rumour, quickly flashed through the crowd, that Fisher and his men were using meat cleavers to chop off people's fingers as they put them through the shutters. A rumour which in the chaos became so strong that several days after the event, some London newspapers were carrying reports that eight human fingers had been found in the sawdust on the shop floor! These reports were later strenuously denied in a statement by Mr Fisher.

In the heat of the moment, however, the rumour served to anger the rioters even more and, by sheer weight of numbers, they forced the shutters open and poured inside, forcing Mr Fisher and his men to beat a swift retreat. The leaders proceeded to pile up furniture and other materials which were then set alight, but the blaze was put out by the fire brigade before getting a hold on the building. Even then, several attempts were made to cut the firemen's hoses.

George Longley took the pillage of his premises more passively, taking no steps to defend his property, except to evacuate his wife and children. It was a shrewd move which probably saved his property from far more damage than the broken windows and fittings his three shops suffered. Instead, he chose to stand and watch as the mob

Flanked by mounted policemen, an assortment of tradesmen's carts and a horse bus, borrowed for the occasion, bring more than thirty men and women from St. Alban's gaol to appear in court on charges arising from the rioting.

proceeded to help itself to the very tempting contents. He studied the faces of the men and women very carefully as they made off with arms full of boots and shoes, rolls of calico, umbrellas, parasols, dresses, hats and hosiery. 'It was noticeable,' he said when giving evidence of identification in court later, 'that the women looters did not hurry but could be seen selecting the refinery with great care.'

By 11.30 p.m., with police reinforcements still on their way by train and horse-drawn vehicle, Superintendent Wood decided to take the only course of action left open to him; he would have to try to recruit a force of Special Constables from the townspeople to deal with the riot, which was, by then, completely out of control. His uniformed men, hopelessly outnumbered, had been attacked and knocked about quite badly. However, before the law allowed him to appeal for civilian volunteers, the Riot Act had to be read—a hazardous task assigned to the magistrate W. T. Coles, who performed it with admirable courage, standing in the Market Place and dodging the occasional lump of wood thrown from the crowd.

'Our Sovereign Lord the King chargeth and commandeth all persons being assembled immediately to disperse themselves and peaceably to depart to their habitations or to their lawful business upon the pains contained in the Act, made in the first year of King George (1714) for preventing tumultuous and riotous assemblies. GOD SAVE THE KING.'

Mr Coles' words could hardly be heard above the din —but that didn't matter; Superintendent Wood had the authority he needed and when he put out his appeal for volunteers he was astonished by the response. Five hundred townsmen of all ages, who had been watching the violence with growing shame and anger, came forward. Of these, two hundred were sworn in straight away, issued with an assortment of official and improvised riot truncheons and divided into several squads, each under the command of a uniformed man. There then began a series of baton charges in which, after several bloody clashes resulting in dozens of split heads, the ringleaders were arrested and the rest of the mob finally broken up at about 3 a.m. Thirty-five people were detained that night, eight of them women, and since there was no room for them in Watford's modest police station, most were taken to St Albans gaol to await their court appearance. Perhaps the most extraordinary feature of the night was that despite the incredible amount of violence, nobody was killed or even critically injured. Inspector Boutell, a sergeant and three policemen received nasty head wounds but none was off duty for more than a few days. Several police horses were stabbed or slashed with sharp instruments, but all survived.

On the Friday morning, the people of Watford emerged to find the town centre in a state of turmoil—the street littered with broken glass, stones, lumps of wood and

On their way to prison. After receiving their prison sentences, ring-leaders of the riot handcuffed in pairs, were taken on a humiliating walk through part of Watford before being put into the wagons that were to take them to prison.

the occasional pool of blood. The volunteer specials, after snatching a couple of hours rest in houses opened to them by grateful residents, were out early on cleaning-up operations and, although they encountered some sporadic stoning from small groups of youths, there was no repetition of the trouble of the previous night. By this time, there had arrived on the scene the Chief Constable of Hertfordshire, Colonel Henry Daniell, and his very able lieutenant, Deputy Chief Constable John Reynolds.

If there is a legendary figure in the Hertfordshire Police Force, it is John Reynolds. A former Superintendent of the Hitchin Division he was an encyclopaedia of police experience; a rigid disciplinarian and the possessor of a fine streak of Hertfordshire cunning which kept him abreast, if not ahead of the movements of most of the county's criminals. He was an autocratic but popular law man who served the Force for the incredible period of fifty-one years. When Mr Reynolds was on the streets there was never any trouble and the people of Watford

93

saw a lot of him during the two very tense days following the riot.

He organised a merciless search of the slum hovels in Ballard's Buildings and Red Lion Yard, where most of the trouble-makers lived. The squads of specials were so thorough that by lunch-time that Friday more arrests had been made, and most of the clothing and footwear looted from Mr Longley's shops had been recovered and piled high in a room at the police station. The search became so hot that many looters panicked and surrendered their individual hauls voluntarily rather than have their homes turned upside down. While all this was going on, Reynolds had taken the precaution of employing the services of a number of carpenters in the town, who spent the day busy at their lathes, turning out dozens of new truncheons!

Later in the day, a strange procession made its way along Watford High Street past the damaged shops to the police court. A horse bus, a wagonette and several tradesmens' carts borrowed for the occasion and each with a couple of policemen aboard, were flanked by more mounted police as the prisoners were brought back from St Albans gaol to appear before a special court. Ironically, only a small proportion of the population was there to witness this procession since most had gone to the railway station, thinking the prisoners would be brought in by train. Fortunately for them, none of the prisoners was charged with offences under the Riot Act, which carried maximum penalties of penal servitude for life. The charges, instead, were confined to assault, larceny and attempted arson. At this and subsequent court hearings forty-six men and eight women were found guilty and received sentences ranging from fines or fourteen days' imprisonment to ten months' hard labour.

On the day when most of the heavier prison sentences were handed out, Deputy Chief Constable Reynolds took the ringleaders on a final humiliating walk through part of the town before putting them into the wagons that carried them off to prison. Handcuffed in pairs and surrounded by a strong force of policemen, they were marched past lines of silent townsfolk. A reporter for the *Watford Observer* watched their journey. 'As they left, they affected an air of bravado,' he wrote. 'But when the last house passed them, their faces changed and more than one was seen to be crying.'

Because the Riot Act had been read, all the victims received full compensation from Town Hall funds, a bill which came to more than £2,000. The two hundred special constables were each given their riot truncheons as a souvenir of the occasion. King Edward got better and on the day of his delayed Coronation the Watford festivities went ahead much as originally planned. It was, however, some years before the town was able to live down the unique and unflattering headlines which it earned during the crisis of King Edward's illness.

9

COUNTRY SCHOOLING—THE STRAW PLAITERS

On the night Sarah Pratt came into the world, her father was turned out of his home to spend the night sleeping under a hedge in the meadow; 4th June, 1842, was a warm night and the village women concerned with the welfare of his wife and baby had scarcely enough room to move about the tiny thatched cottage as it was. Thomas Pratt didn't mind a night in the fields anyway, since he spent most of his life there, for Thomas, like 90 per cent of the men in the village of Pirton, was an agricultural labourer. Yet, although he earned only 7s. 6d. a week, he was not worried by the prospect of another mouth to feed and another body to clothe; for in his village the wives and the children between them earned twice as much in a week as their men could bring home.

The reason was geographical. Pirton was one of many poor farming communities within the twenty mile radius of Luton, and Luton, since the end of the 17th century, had been a thriving centre of the nation's hat industry. Most hats and bonnets were made of straw and, before it could be used, the straw had to be plaited; millions of yards of it every year. Since there were no machines to do the work it was done by hand and for two hundred years this provided a cottage industry that gave the poor of North Hertfordshire and South Bedfordshire a standard of living well above the appalling conditions endured in other parts of the country.

By the time Sarah was born, the craft had progressed well beyond early plaiting techniques which produced only a rather broad, coarse plait. Small hand-tools called straw-splitters—invented by the French plaiters of

Village girls from Hertfordshire and Bedfordshire at a Plait Trade Fair at Luton in 1885. The girl with the large coil of plait over one arm is negotiating a price with the plait dealer, who would then have sold it to a hat manufacturer. It was not unusual for a girl to complete as much as 240 yards of plait in a week.

Tuscany—were used to split each straw into several strips, which resulted in a finer plait as narrow as a quarter of an inch. The peak of the plaiting season was between the months of December and May leading up to the spring sales period and during that time it dominated village life.

Almost every evening during those months the three generations of each family gathered round the fire in their cottages to work in the light of tallow candles with the plait straw, cut into ten-inch lengths, in a jug of water on the table to keep it moist and supple. Nothing was allowed to interfere—fretful babies were drugged into silence with *Godfrey's*, a tranquilliser containing opium. Those parents unwilling or unable to afford the marketed product poured into their offspring a crude imitation which they had made themselves by boiling poppy heads in water.

Thomas Pratt's family didn't go to these extremes.

97

Though poor, they were also extremely religious and, because both mother and father could read and write, were regarded as scholars. Consequently, while Sarah was taught to plait from the age of three, her parents also laid equal emphasis on teaching her the Bible and how to read and write. They never worked on a Sunday. This was spent at the Baptist Chapel and in enjoying the more refined tasks of sewing and embroidery. As a result Sarah enjoyed a considerable advantage over her friends when, at the age of 5, she was sent to the Plaiting School.

The Plaiting School was another phenomenon of the hat industry; a highly organised form of child labour run under the guise of education. Every village around Luton had a Plaiting School and every poor child went there. Each school was supervised by a woman who was supposed to teach reading, writing, arithmetic and plaiting; the idea being that the children could be educated while earning money at the same time; a form of child labour far less vile than that employed in the factories and the coal mines, but child labour nevertheless.

At one time, thirteen thousand children were going to schools such as these. Their parents paid 2d. a week for the schooling, supplied their own straw and were allowed to sell their child's plait afterwards. Since there was never any check on the qualifications of the women who ran these places many degenerated into miniature plait factories with a woman overseer in charge who could neither read nor write. In some areas, after six hours plaiting (with a lunch-break) during the day, the children would be sent back by their parents after tea for another three-hour 'evening class'.

At the same time, many of these schools were run as originally intended and Sarah Pratt was fortunate enough to go to one of them. She became the top girl of her class and a skilled plaiter, so that by the time she was 13 she could contribute as much to the family income as her mother and grandmother. They were paid 10d. a score and, since a score was twenty yards they could, by plait-ing 240 yards a week, earn 10s. 0d. each. In fact, to plait this length of straw was not unusual because in time the young women learned to plait instinctively. They took it with them on walks, they plaited while they read or while they rocked the baby to sleep.

Once a week Sarah or her mother would walk the three miles into Hitchin to sell their work to the visiting Luton plait dealers who came to the market. It was always an exciting morning of hard bargaining; the wary dealers making sure they weren't being sold short measure, the women looking for the dealer offering the best price and impressing on him the high quality of their work. Then, they had to buy more straw from straw dealers, who cut and bleached the straw ready for plaiting.

Apart from two years away in London, which she didn't like, Sarah earned a livelihood from straw-plaiting for nearly forty years. She also became a casualty of the slump in the demand for home-made plait which

A buzzing scene of activity in 1865 that Sarah Thrussell knew well. The Tuesday morning straw-plait market at Hitchin, where as much as £1,000-worth of business was done during the day. Village women gather and gossip as they await the arrival of the plait dealers from Luton. The bundle which each woman carries represents the week's work of her family.

Sarah Thrussell (1842–1934) straw-plaiting at her cottage in Pirton, Hertfordshire. As a young woman she could earn as much as 10s od. a week, more than her father could earn for seven days' labouring on a farm.

developed towards the end of the century. It was a decline caused partly by the revolution in the manufacture of felt hats, which brought their prices to within range of most people, but mainly by the import of good quality plait which the Japanese somehow managed to sell to Britain, not at 10d. a score but 3d., so displaying early signs of a talent for cut-price imitation that was to be repeated later with cigarette lighters, transistor radios and television sets.

Sarah spent some years supplementing the dwindling income from plaiting by working as a housekeeper and nurse for some of her wealthier friends in the Baptist Church. Then she received a proposal of marriage from William Thrussell, the village cobbler. She accepted, bore him a son and lived to be 90.

Sarah Thrussell accepted the end of the straw-plaiting era philosophically, which is more than can be said for some of her neighbours. A notable cause of uproar was the introduction of compulsory education in the 1870s which, at the same time, banned straw-plaiting in schools. The move was decidedly unpopular with many parents who not only lost a sizeable chunk of their weekly income but had to continue paying the 2d. a week for schooling. It was a small crisis well illustrated by the remarks entered in the School Log Book by the new schoolmaster at Pirton in the autumn of 1877:

'October—several of the elder children still absent gleaning. . . . Many children not paid their school fees. Sent them back for their money but didn't get it. . . . Several of the infants have commenced attending only half time, being kept at home to plait. . . . Mrs B. kept Fred at home all day rather than pay 2d. . . . November 28th. INVESTED IN A CANE FOR THE FIRST TIME.'

10

A PUBLIC ENQUIRY—
THE TRAIN ACCIDENTS

The astonishing disclosures of negligence made after the
Hitchin to Royston train disaster in 1866 were more
than enough to provoke a national scandal. The fact that
the event was accepted as little more than 'an unfortunate accident' reveals a good deal about the extraordinary
lack of concern shown by Victorian travellers over the
hair-raising incidents that were occurring almost daily on
their railways.

The train was the morning express from King's Cross
to Cambridge. When it pulled out of Hitchin station at
10.20 a.m. on 3rd July it was running only a minute or
two late. In the second class carriages immediately behind the engine were groups of workmen, some employed
by the Great Northern Railway Company, others on their
way to put up telegraph lines. In the two first class
carriages which followed were a few passengers destined
mainly for Royston and Cambridge. The first ten miles
of the journey were uneventful; the train stopped at
Ashwell and then trundled on along the Hertfordshire
border towards Royston.

About two miles from the town, when it was approaching the Litlington level crossing the train, according to
passengers' statements later, was 'travelling at its normal
speed of about 30 miles an hour'. Suddenly, the engine
lurched violently to the left and jumped the rails; it
careered along the track for eighty yards and then rolled
down the embankment, turning over twice before coming
to rest on its wheels in a field of barley. Although the
coupling between the engine and the second class carriages
broke away, the jolt was severe enough to throw them

The wrecked engine, with guard's van, brought back to Hitchin for examination.

off the track as well and they also overturned, trapping the workmen inside. The impact on the first class carriages was rather less and, although derailed, they stayed upright.

Arthur Nash, a lawyer from Royston, was in one of these carriages and, with several fellow passengers, he jumped out on to the track and ran to give help. He found the engine driver, Andrew Hunter, aged 25, and his stoker William Clarke, aged 31, lying in the field both dying from fearful head injuries. Realising there was nothing they could do to help the crew, Nash and the others set to work to free the nine workmen, still trapped in the crushed remains of the second class carriage. They managed to release all the men who, although seriously injured, survived their ordeal. Having seen the casualties away to hospital, Arthur Nash turned his attention to the railway track and his findings formed an important part of the evidence at the inquest on the dead railwaymen.

'I examined the track,' he said, 'and some of the sleepers

were very rotten indeed. I saw men kick the rotten wood away.' Other early indications of the appalling state of this section of the line were given by the widows of the dead train crew. Mrs Ellen Hunter recalled: 'My husband had remarked many times how tired he was after travelling over this stretch of line, from having been shaken about so much.' The stoker's widow, Hannah Clarke, told the coroner that her husband had declared on several occasions that it was not safe to travel on that section of the track. The inquest was then adjourned for an official Board of Trade investigation by Captain W. H. Tyler of the Royal Engineers and when his report was presented several days later, the evidence of earlier witnesses was more than confirmed.

'Looking from the point of the accident towards Hitchin,' the Captain reported, 'one could see the rails were in a wavy condition for a distance of 220 yards.' It was not difficult for him to explain this condition either, since not only were most of the wooden sleepers 'in the last stages of rottenness'—but also there were only half as many under each section of rail as there should have been! Nor were the rails properly fitted; they were sitting in loose clamps which had been fixed to the sleepers with an assortment of spikes and nails. There were not even any 'fish-plates', those essential standard fittings used to bolt the end of each section of rail to the next! Not unnaturally, the constant pounding of successive trains on the loose rail ends had caused numerous chips in the rails themselves.

The Captain also made a thorough inspection of the ill-fated engine after it had been taken back to the sheds at Hitchin. It was, he discovered, a single-tank engine of a kind which should never have been used to pull a passenger train since—because of its weight and design—it would have run less steadily, particularly on such a bad track as the one between Hitchin and Royston. Captain Tyler also discovered that one of the main suspension

Hitchin Railway station in 1865.

springs in the engine had been fractured for a considerable time before the accident and this had apparently
gone unnoticed the last time it was serviced. So he
deduced that the bad state of the track and the unsteadi-
ness of the engine with the fractured spring had combined
to cause it to jump the rails with disastrous results.

Having decided how the accident was caused, Captain
Tyler went on to interview the senior engineers of both
the Great Northern and Great Eastern Railway Companies to try to establish how it was that the track had
reached this state of neglect. It turned out that until 1st
April, 1866 (eight weeks before the accident), the line had
belonged to the Great Eastern Railway Company, and
their engineer had examined it in December 1865 and had
ordered 11,400 new sleepers to be inserted in the per-
manent way. Clearly, he wasn't worried by a sense of
urgency, since when Great Northern acquired the line
four months later none of the work had been done, and

the 11,400 sleepers were handed over to the succeeding company for them to put in. Great Northern's engineer appears to have regarded the need for track repairs as rather more urgent and workmen began laying the new sleepers almost straight away. By July, of the eighteen miles of double track ear-marked for repair, eleven had been completed, but that unfortunately did not include the worst section near the Litlington level crossing.

However, Captain Tyler's report concluded on a note of reassurance. 'I am glad to learn,' he wrote, 'that in addition to the greatly increased force of men which was employed after the line was taken over in April, the numbers have been still further augmented so that the re-laying of the whole eighteen miles may be completed in twelve weeks. The joints of the rails and the fastenings should in the meantime be very carefully attended to. Orders have wisely been given to slacken the speed of trains, pending the completion of this re-laying; and posts have been erected and wires strained for providing tele-graphic communications which, strange to say, had not previously been supplied.'

What then, following these disturbing disclosures, did the coroner and jury have to say? In short, very little. There were no public reprimands for Great Northern for failing to impose a strict speed limit earlier on a section of track they must have known was highly dangerous; there was no criticism, beyond Captain Tyler's mild re-bukes, about the use of a badly maintained and incorrect engine to haul a passenger train. Incredibly, nobody seems to have seen fit to publicly condemn the appalling track maintenance record of the Great Eastern Company who, in the fourteen years during which they had been responsible for the line, had allowed it to deteriorate to a point of total collapse and even then had done nothing positive about it. Neither was this the first crash on their section of the Cambridge branch line. Only a month earlier there had been another serious derailment between Royston and Cambridge. At the enquiry into the earlier incident the engine driver (having been lucky enough to escape with his life) told another Board of Trade inspector that he had complained to a superior about the weakness and danger of the track, but nothing had been done.

The jury at Royston, meanwhile, were unanimous in returning a verdict of accidental death on the crew of the tank engine, echoing Captain Tyler's remarks that, as the line was unsafe, it would be 'imprudent' to run trains at such a high rate of speed. Far from wishing to offer any criticism of the railway companies they chose instead to 'highly commend' the Great Northern Railway for the improvements they were making, which they were sure would eventually make the line 'one of the soundest in the kingdom.'

By Victorian standards the outcome of the Hitchin to Royston train disaster was not unusual and the men of the district who adjudicated at the enquiry were merely reflecting a nationwide attitude that was prevalent at the time. In 1866, the railways were still developing and were regarded as a new and exciting means of transport. The rival railway companies having invested vast sums of money in laying ten thousand miles of track were concerned not so much with safety but with getting better returns from faster and more efficient services. Because it was still too early for a national code of safety to have been developed, each company had its own standards which, only painful experience was to prove, were completely inadequate. It seems unbelievable, for example, that these companies were running trains capable of 60 miles an hour with no brakes beyond a primitive wooden block system on the engine wheels, operated by hand! This, coupled with highly unreliable signalling systems, set a predictable course for rail disasters, which happened with horrifying regularity.

In 1866, Captain Tyler and three colleagues from the Board of Trade investigated no fewer than eighty major rail accidents in the United Kingdom, many far worse than the Hitchin to Royston disaster. There were two more in Hertfordshire that same year. On 9th June, three goods trains were involved in a collision inside Welwyn tunnel, resulting in the deaths of two railwaymen and injury to two others. A neglectful guard and a poor signalling system were blamed. On 11th October twelve passengers sitting in a stationary train at Hitchin station were injured when a goods train, mercifully travelling at under 10 miles an hour, rammed it from behind. The driver of the goods train was fined.

Contemporary accounts of these disasters show that public concern for better safety standards was only temporarily aroused if members of the public were themselves actually killed or maimed. The deaths of railwaymen were regarded as rather more inevitable. Reports of accidents frequently made the point—not 'unfortunately the crew was killed' but 'fortunately *only* the crew was killed'. This casual approach to the high mortality rate among railwaymen was a point taken up with some force by the editor of *Railway Gazette* in the Christmas issue in 1866.

After dutifully listing the progress and profits of the various railway companies the editor went on to reveal some statistics which they, no doubt, would have preferred to have left buried. The previous year the companies had paid out more than £330,000 in compensation to some of the victims of railway disasters or their dependants. In all, 221 people had died and 1,132 had been injured—and of the dead more than half were railwaymen. 'The companies,' the editor wrote, 'are not compelled by law to send a note of such trifles to the Board of Trade (on the principle we presume that they are entitled to do what they like with their own) and it may be safely concluded that this list is very far from complete. The causes of all this slaughter and maiming demand a separate investigation.'

It was, however, many years before the Board of Trade was able to pressure the powerful railway chiefs to think as much about safety regulations as they did about profits. Although these men were often guilty of negligence, it was not always deliberate negligence. The regulations may have been primitive but they were made, for the most part, by men with a high sense of responsibility. Their failures were, more often than not, caused simply by a lack of experience. A frequent remark heard from train drivers and engineers at Board of Trade enquiries or inquests was 'I never believed it could have happened'. Time after time, events proved that it could. Most railway companies were prepared to accept the findings and recommendations which came out of these enquiries; the trouble was, that advice came too late to benefit the victims at whose inquest it was given.

Andrew Hunter and William Clarke were just two out of hundreds who died before the autocratic Victorian pioneers of Britain's railways finally acknowledged that power and speed were no good without the equipment and regulations to control them.

11

A CRAFTSMAN'S LIFE—THE WHEELWRIGHT

William Wilson was the last of a family line that had supplied the farming community of Breachwood Green, King's Walden and thereabouts with a transport system for well over one hundred and fifty years, and when his customers and friends no longer had need of such temporal forms of mobility as the farm cart or the trap, he made coffins and organised 'with full and solemn dignity' their final transportation to the burial ground. William Wilson discovered early on that there was far more to a wheelwright's job than making wheels. He also had to learn how to make ladders, mend a roof, paint a sign and decorate a sitting room. So wide were the demands made by what were then quite isolated communities, that his work frequently demanded not only the skill of a carpenter but also the eye of an artist and the physical endurance of a cart-horse.

All that old Samuel Wilson had learned as an apprentice to his father in the late 1830s, was passed on to William. As soon as he was old enough, the boy was taken to the timber sales, held in the woods on the big estates in Hertfordshire and Bedfordshire, where the wheelwrights and the timber merchants would gather to bid for the mature trees the estate was offering for sale. There, William learned to assess the quality of each variety. Oak, Ash, Beech, Elm, Pine, and Fir. He learned to gauge from the shape of the trunk, those trees which would provide the most timber for their work, and those which had the best upper branches for fire-logs and faggot-wood. He watched as his father's mark was put on the trunk of the growing tree he had purchased and which,

William Wilson, wheelwright, at the age of 30 and dressed for Chapel.

Old Samuel Wilson, about 1885, wearing his favourite moleskin skull cap, stands by one of the large two-wheeled farm carts which he and his son made. In the barn behind, a ladder recently completed.

next winter when the sap was at its lowest, he would have to help fell.

The journey back to their yard at Breachwood Green was often a long one. The smaller logs cut on the site, were no problem, but the huge trunk was a different matter. It meant hiring William Taylor's massive timber gig, with a team of four horses, from King's Walden, and possibly employing extra hands. Once at the yard, there began the tricky job of getting the trunk over the sawpit, using a complicated but highly efficient system of ropes, iron levers and log rollers.

The Wilson's sawpit was in a long open-ended barn— a pit thirty feet long and eight feet deep, across which the newly felled trunk had to be supported by a number of rollers and iron pins. Here, William learned from his father how to mark out the trunk geometrically with chalk in a way that would enable them to extract the largest amount of useful timber. Then began the back-breaking work with the eight-foot long, double-handed pit-saw, as the trunk was cut into sections lengthways. Of the two men using the saw, it was always reckoned that the one down in the pit had an easier time than the one on top, because he pulled downwards on his cutting stroke while his mate above him had to pull up, which was a somewhat harder task. The sawdust that cascaded down on him, getting into his eyes, up his nose and under the clothing that clung to his sweating body, was considered a minor inconvenience, though things became more unpleasant after heavy rain when the bottom of the saw-pit was water-logged. The timber obtained during these long and arduous sessions in the sawpit then had to be stacked under a corrugated iron roof, designed to keep it dry while still allowing the air to reach it during the several years it was left to season.

The wheels they made, varied in size and shape according to the type of wagon or cart they were making. The technique they used was fairly primitive by modern

Ready to move off—a heavy timber gig in Old Watling Street, Radlett, at about the turn of the century.

engineering standards, so their achievements were all the more remarkable. With no machines to cut accurate pre-set patterns, nor even any drawings, they made each wheel by 'feel', each one an individual masterpiece of precision. The axle-box, a cylinder of iron, was set just-so into a stock of elm to form the hub that would slide on to the axle on which the wheel revolved. A fraction of an inch out of true and the completed wagon would wander from side to side 'looking into everyone's windows all down street'. The spokes, each shaved from oak, were set into holes carefully chiselled into the hub. Then came the felloes, the sections making up the outer ring of the wheel, made, like the hub, from elm.

With each wheel completed, William and his father would turn to the forge, where they fashioned the bonds for metal tyres, each one of which was made deliberately

Wheelwrights at work—father and son. In their yard at Breachwood Green at the turn of the century, Samuel Wilson holds the metal wedge with pincers as his son William makes ready to strike a worn metal tyre from the wheel of a local farm wagon. Behind them, a lightweight gig which they had recently completed and which would probably have cost the buyer about £15.

an inch or so smaller than the outside rim of the wooden wheel. In a roaring wood fire, each was heated until white hot and then carried on rods across to the circular platform on which the cartwheel lay. Having expanded with the heat to a size slightly larger than the wheel, it was tapped into position in a cloud of smoke and flame as the heat began to scorch the wooden felloes. This part of the operation called for extreme speed and accuracy. Once satisfied that the tyre was in position, the wheelwrights poured on water which replaced the smoke with a great plume of hissing steam as the tyre contracted to grip the felloes and tongues of the spokes tighter than any vice.

William and his father supplied vehicles for almost every section of the agricultural industry; the big four-wheeled wagons that took the sheaves from field to farm and the corn from farm to mill; the lighter two-wheeled carts and the dainty light-weight traps, beautifully varnished and upholstered. They made the water-carts, vast barrels on wheels, and the four-wheeled Shepherds'

115

Huts, simple but effective caravans in which the shepherds lived during the lambing season. Around harvest time, there was the inevitable repair work when, on a particularly hot day, the temperature, combined with friction from the road, often caused the metal tyres to work loose and come off; which meant that the wheelwrights had to be up at 4 a.m. next morning to light the forge and re-fix the rims in time for work the same day. As the heat caused one problem, so the cold caused another. The wax for coffin polishing needs to be warm and soft to work in well. William's workshop had no heating which meant coffin-waxing was out of the question on a frosty day. So on cold nights he took his work home with him to finish it in the warmth of his dining room after the supper dishes had been cleared from the table.

The nature of their work kept father and son superbly fit. The tree-felling, the sawpit and the forge obliged them to perform as routine feats of physical endurance what the pampered body of today's average working man would be quite unable to sustain. It was a stamina reflected in William's favourite recreation of cycling, and illustrated by the fact that one weekend in 1890 he mounted his heavy Penny Farthing with solid tyres and pedalled the rough roads to Brighton and back; a round trip of one hundred and seventy miles.

In fact, the bicycle and the later introduction of the circular saw to his timber yard, were about the only forms of modern mechanisation that William Wilson was prepared to accept into his way of life. After Samuel died in 1910 at the age of 84, William carried on the business in much the same way as his father had conducted it during the Victorian age. His marriage had given him two daughters but no son and so he was obliged to take on a number of apprentices during the next thirty years.

It is perhaps not a bad thing that, as William's long life went into decline so, too, did the demand for his craft. Fate made him the last of his line and yet was kind enough to assure sufficient work until he no longer needed it. He never drove a car and celebrated his 80th birthday by buying a new bicycle, and even after that, continued to work in a modest way until failing eyesight forced him to give up. We met once at the house in Coleman's Road which he built for his bride at the turn of the century. He was bemoaning the fact that the recent operation on his eyes hadn't done a lot of good. It had, in fact, improved his vision but had not restored the keenness and clarity of sight which he remembered. He talked for more than an hour, giving me a detailed insight into Victorian and Edwardian life in his village and indicating quite clearly his profound sympathy for the unfortunate lads of Breachwood Green who now had to earn their living by 'going to Luton and pulling a lever in a factory all day', instead of being able to enjoy the challenges and completeness of a craft such as his own. It was a rather sweeping generalisation, but I understood what he meant.

William Wilson died in 1956 at the age of 91. Mercifully, it was well before Luton Corporation extended the runway of the airport just across the fields from his house. The airliners that now thunder past his parlour window every few minutes on their missions to some package tour paradise would have been too much for the old man who found a lifetime of fulfilment from craftmanship in wood.

12

THE FORGOTTEN VISIONARY

On a summer afternoon in 1906 the villagers of Shenley in Hertfordshire were startled out of their wits by the sight of a machine which, so far as Edwardian England was concerned, belonged only to the science-fiction world of H. G. Wells. The sleek lines resembled those of a modern racing car and the grey armour-plated body was surmounted by a rotating turret from which protruded two sinister machine guns. As it clattered to a halt in a cloud of dust, a flap at the front opened, and out scrambled a crowd of noisy and very frightened chickens.

In time, the people living in the country areas between Barnet and St Albans became used to such happenings and, for the most part, came to regard them with amusement; none realised that what they were witnessing was the work of a remarkable pioneer of the British Cinema Industry, a man who in many ways was years ahead of his time, but whose naïvety in what, even then, was a hard business world, caused him to become one of the cinema's forgotten men.

Arthur Melbourne-Cooper was born at St Albans in 1874, the son of the city's first and most successful portrait photographer, Thomas Melbourne-Cooper. As a boy he learned the art of photography from his father the hard way, spending many hours a week coating glass plates with emulsion or printing orders in the dark room while his friends were out at play. It was an unofficial apprenticeship which paid off, for by the time he was 18, young Melbourne-Cooper was an accomplished still photographer, ready to embark on a career which even in Victorian times, was considered a very respectable profession. It was with this background that, in 1892, he applied

Arthur Melbourne-Cooper in 1907.

for a job as assistant to a Barnet man, Birt Acres, who at this time was reaching an exciting stage in experiments with a camera he had designed to take moving pictures. As with the men who developed the art of still photography some fifty years earlier, there is controversy even today over precisely who should be accredited with which invention—though it is fair to say that Acres was at this time working almost in parallel with the more celebrated pioneers of motion pictures, Thomas Edison in America and the Lumiere brothers in France and, as such, can be described as one of the early pioneers of the British cinema. In fact, the practical development of the motion picture in Britain is dated from the granting of a patent to Acres in May 1895 for a combined cine-camera and projector with appliance for loop-forming. He had worked on this equipment with Robert Paul, a Hatton Garden optical-instrument maker, who later claimed that the country's very first film presentation using this equipment took place in his workshop. It was a claim which provoked a whole series of arguments and acrimonious debates.

However, throughout this time Arthur Melbourne-Cooper was working as Birt Acres' assistant, operating the new equipment on a series of assignments around the country. In 1895 they filmed The Derby, the Boat Race and the Henley Royal Regatta, becoming the first newsreel men to record people and scenes from everyday life. At the end of the year they assembled a collection of their films and on 14th January, 1896, gave what is now the first *recorded* public screening of motion pictures in Britain—before members of the Royal Photographic Society in London. In the same year, Acres took their films and his Kineopticon, as he called it, to Marlborough House where a dinner party was being held to celebrate the approaching wedding of Princess Maud and Prince Charles of Denmark. The show, commanded by the Prince of Wales (later King Edward VII), was seen by more than forty crowned heads of Europe and can be described as the first Royal Command Film Performance.

In fact, film shows during this period were not just the prerogative of photographic experts and royalty. Many ordinary men and women in Hertfordshire were given unexpected previews during 1895–96 as Acres and Melbourne-Cooper sought to try out the Kineopticon on a live audience in preparation for the more important viewings later on. One such event was held in Barnet Town Hall and included film of the Barnet Militia on parade in the town. For this epic, Melbourne-Cooper was deputed to stand behind the screen and add sound effects by blowing a bugle! Melbourne-Cooper himself claims to have given a show at Welham Green Boys' School, North Mimms during Christmas 1895, when villagers saw a series of local scenes and comedy episodes performed for the cameraman by some of the more extrovert locals. One —A Study in Black and White— showed a man throwing flour over another, who retaliated by throwing soot.

In these very early days none of the films shown was longer than fifty feet and each lasted only a couple of minutes. The conditions under which they were shown were sufficient to chill the heart of any present-day fire safety officer. The fire risk involved must have been substantial as excited villagers crowded into their tiny hall, packed around the projector and its highly-inflammable film—a projector lit, not by electricity but by a very bright gas jet supplied by gas from a pressure bag on the floor nearby. It was quite a common occurrence as the performance wore on and the gas light began to dim, for Melbourne-Cooper to brighten the picture by getting a number of small boys to sit on the gas bag to squeeze the last ounce of gas towards the burning jet.

Melbourne-Cooper and Birt Acres were men of very different personalities. Acres was a scientist, an inventor whose interest in the new medium was much more academic than commercial. Melbourne-Cooper, on the other hand, was an artist with a natural sense of humour who, even at this time, saw a great future for motion pictures as a source of entertainment and towards the end of the century he began freelance camera work for some of the handful of pioneer film companies which were beginning to get established in London. He claimed to be the first man in Britain to make an advertising film when, in 1897, he shot a film for Bird's Custard Powder. It was simple and, as with most of his work, contained a degree of humour. It showed a contemporary Bird's poster coming to life; an old man walked downstairs carrying a tray of eggs. Predictably, he tripped over, smashing them. The message was that he had no cause to worry because—he used Bird's Custard Powder. Two years later he made what is believed to be the earliest surviving British advertising film, sponsored by Bryant and May and taking the form of an appeal to the public to buy matches to send to troops fighting in the Boer War.

It was for this film that he used a technique for which he is now acknowledged as a pioneer—animation—or the use of a series of single-frame exposures of models to create a sequence of moving pictures. He made a box of Bryant and May matches open up and the contents pop out one at a time and march like soldiers to form a ladder to a blackboard where one 'wrote' the message:

'For one guinea Messrs Bryant and May will forward a case containing sufficient to supply a box of matches to each man in a battalion: with the name of the sender inside.'

Up to 1900 there were few places of entertainment prepared to show films regularly. The Music Hall managers called them 'chasers-out' because they found audiences leaving after the live show, apparently not interested in the films. A few London theatres staged performances of films showing important events but, for the most part, these now-priceless records of late Victorian

The earliest surviving British advertising film. A still from Bryant and May's appeal to buy matches for troops fighting in the Boer War —made by Melbourne-Cooper in 1899.

life had only one regular outlet—to the fairgrounds, where the more enterprising showmen saw them as a bigger money-spinner than the traditional peepshows which normally occupied so many fairground booths. Melbourne-Cooper once recalled that he received no basic fee for making an advertisement film, only £1 from the sponsors for every copy he could get shown at a fairground.

It was because of his determination to lift the film industry from this lowly status of fairground booths that he decided in 1901 to set up his own film-making company in his home town of St Albans, with a long-term plan to establish a cinema there as a place of entertainment in its own right. He formed a company called Alpha Cinematograph Films and launched himself into a career which was astonishing not only for its introduction of new camera techniques but also for its prolific output. In a matter of a year or two, Arthur Melbourne-Cooper became a figure known and respected throughout the industry; a founder-member of the Kinematograph

Manufacturers' Association he found his services in almost daily demand.

He derived enormous benefit from an episode in 1903 when he was commissioned by the Duke of Devonshire to go to Chatsworth House, in Derbyshire, to film a garden party given for King Edward VII and Queen Alexandra. He astonished the guests by developing the film and showing it in the ballroom the same evening. 'A record in such matters in connection with a private house', the Court Correspondent of the *Daily Telegraph* reported the following morning. Later the same year he persuaded the London and North-Western Railway to allow him to convert a coach into a dark room and went up to Liverpool to film the Grand National. By processing the film in the coach on the way back to London he was able to show it to an audience at the Empire Theatre, Leicester Square, at 10.45 p.m. the same evening.

In 1904 he made a drama called *Rescue in Mid-Air* using actors and puppets and achieved a sequence (emulated many years later in *Mary Poppins*) in which a young nursemaid, stranded up a church tower, floated to safety with the help of an umbrella. He pioneered hilarious screen chases, using motor cars, clowns and comic police-men some years before the arrival of that classic American film comedy team the Keystone Cops. He even made a horror film, *Resurrection of Rameses*, in which an Egyptian mummy came to life and terrorised the local inhabitants—but the distributors considered it too horrific and he was unable to sell it either in Britain or America.

His film *The Motor Pirate*, of which clips still survive, is now generally regarded as one of his masterpieces. He constructed around his own car the futuristic tank which alarmed the residents of Shenley and thereabouts so much, and devised the story of a mechanised monster which rumbled through the countryside devouring all that came within its path. To obtain this effect, chickens were put into a crate in the front of the vehicle and then filmed as the hatch opened and they scrambled out. The operation was repeated with a policeman tumbling out of the front. However, the camera used to take these pictures was upside down, so that when the film was processed and added to the rest of the film back-to-front, the audience saw the sequence in reverse, with chickens and policeman being apparently sucked into the machine.

By this time, Alpha Studios were producing almost a film a day including documentaries on fishing boats and the Royal Mint, short comedies, animated cartoons, almost everything upon which the cinema industry of today is based. His *Dream of Toyland*, employing dolls, toy animals, miniature cars and buses in a street set built in his studios, sold well over three hundred copies, including more than seventy to America. By 1908 his business was earning a lot of money and he was able to fulfil the final part of his early ambitions. The studio property which he rented in Alma Road extended over two acres and it was here that he converted an old Polytechnic building into the Alpha Picture Palace—the first British picture palace to have a sloping and separate projection booth, and also the first to depart from the standard theatre practice of charging more for the seats at the front than for those at the rear. It was an innovation which attracted comment in the industry's leading trade magazine *The Bioscope*:

'It is a feature worthy of note,' wrote the visitor, 'That the lower priced places are in front and the better ones at the back. This arrangement was somewhat resented at first by the patrons of the higher priced seats, but when they found that the specially-raised floor gave them a better view than could be got from the front, they appreciated the innovation. The operator's box does not stand in the usual place inside the auditorium. It is a roomy apartment built out as an annex, and therefore affords immunity from accident as well as from interference from the public.'

Alpha Studios were, by this time, working flat out, seven days a week. Melbourne-Cooper who, up to now, had not only filmed but acted in many of his productions, was obliged to concentrate on the business side and employ more technicians, authors and professional actors on a regular basis. Men and women working on the West End stage would take an early morning train out to St Albans to spend several hours acting in the quaint silent dramas and comedies at the studios. Many were performed on a revolving set which Melbourne-Cooper had designed so that it could be turned to face the sun as the day progressed. Other scenes, including many chase-sequences, were shot in the streets of St Albans itself, the actresses having to put up with a barrage of ribald remarks from crowds of young lads gathered to watch the filming. Some of these often had to be ejected forcibly from the set as they tried to get in on the act. A full-length film, of around five hundred feet, would be completed in a couple of days, despite the distractions and the problems caused by the capricious weather. Many actors jumped at the chance to take part—they welcomed the change from stage performances and the pay (7s. 6d. a day, with railway fare and lunch thrown in) was considered very handsome.

The year that Arthur Melbourne-Cooper opened the Alpha Picture Palace was also the year that the cinema, as we know it today, really arrived in Britain—despite the popular theory that it was not until the Great War that it became a socially-acceptable form of entertainment. It had achieved the status of a major industry well before the end of the Edwardian era. From 1908 onwards there was a burst of activity in towns and cities throughout the South, the Midlands and the North as old public halls, variety theatres, shops and even warehouses were hastily converted into picture palaces. By 1912 there were four

A clip from an early comedy film with Arthur Melbourne-Cooper playing a postman during a chase sequence.

thousand in the British Isles, though few were of the high quality of the St Albans cinema. Many were small with only narrow benches for seating and the absolute minimum of decoration and comfort. Melbourne-Cooper's had quite exotic decor, coloured electric arc-lighting and a refreshment lounge. Nevertheless, whatever standards they offered, each was an outlet for all the popular films of the day, thus contributing to the growth of the industry.

If 1908–09 was the year of the growth of the British cinema, it was also the year that marked the beginning of the decline of Arthur Melbourne-Cooper's distinguished career. That decline was signalled by his opening a second Picture Palace in Letchworth Garden City, the dream town of Sir Ebenezer Howard, where the arrival of such a frivolous institution was far from welcome. During his negotiations to rent a property in the town Melbourne-Cooper received a curt note from one council official telling him that neither his picture palace nor his noisy car was welcome in the Garden City! He persevered, though, giving a number of free performances in an effort to win over the local population, and the Letchworth Picture Palace opened in 1909, but it never made any money for Melbourne-Cooper.

From that point on, the St Albans cinema pioneer went deeper and deeper into troubled financial waters. He owned none of the properties from which he ran his studios and cinemas and, as his debts mounted, the crisis point was reached in 1911 when he, his wife and two small daughters were evicted by court bailiffs from their house, and all their personal effects seized—all, that is, except for a small amount of family silver which Melbourne-Cooper's wife, Kate, smuggled out in bags concealed beneath her petticoat. During the next three years the family lived in the London area; Melbourne-Cooper found work and made one more attempt to establish an independent film-making and exhibition company. It had its head office in Warwick Court, Holborn, and when it, too, ran into debt and the rates on the property fell into serious arrears, Arthur Melbourne-Cooper was taken to court and sentenced to a month in Brixton Prison. It was an undignified exit and a rather unjust ending to a career which had contributed so much to the growth of the British cinema for, from that point on, Melbourne-Cooper and his reputation began to slip from public memory.

At first, it may be difficult to imagine how this could happen in view of the staggering output of the Alpha Studios during the preceding decade. It would seem that Melbourne-Cooper's films, at least, should have kept his name before the public eye. The trouble was that his business aptitude was so lacking that he didn't think of establishing any form of copyright on his productions. He sent them off to the distributors and agents unmarked, leaving the more astute among them to add their own trademarks later on. As a result many of the miniature masterpieces which Arthur Melbourne-Cooper created were credited to other people in later years.

There is little doubt, too, that his downfall can be attributed partly to the social attitudes of the time. Consider the impact which the opening of a film studio would have on a small, close-knit Edwardian community such as St Albans. Here was the son of their most respected portrait photographer suddenly bringing into their midst a circus of people who one normally associated only with the suspect 'gay life' of the big cities. London actresses—nicknamed, unfairly by some '*The Alpha Harem*'—cavorting about the streets of a cathedral city, making films for the hoi-polloi of the fairgrounds! Nobody actually voiced any criticism in public but the disapproval was there, beneath the surface. This suspicion of moving pictures and the tales they told is well illustrated by an episode which occurred in a local Congregational Church Hall, to which Melbourne-Cooper had been invited to present a show. He took with him a fairly standard selection of one-reelers which included one entitled *What the Farmer Saw*. This was a piece of the mildest Edwardian titillation, in which a farmer, looking through a telescope, sees a young couple out on a bicycle ride. The young lady appears in some distress as a button on her boot has become undone. Her beau gallantly bends down to help and there is a close-up view of the lady's booted ankle. That was all—but when the film reached this point on the night it was shown in the Congregational Hall, the performance was ended abruptly. The local lay preacher, worried lest his flock should be corrupted, had jumped up and hastily hung his cap over the lens of the projector!

The motion picture is the only truly new art form to emerge this century. Melbourne-Cooper was something

129

of a visionary whose creative mind had been quick to exploit it as a means of communication and entertainment, in the certainty that one day it would become accepted as a part of everyday life. Like so many artists who have tried to place something new and rather revolutionary before a cautious public he was treated with a certain amount of suspicion and gentle contempt; regarded as an eccentric who was dabbling in some brief technical gimmickry in which even the fairground masses would lose interest one day. Consequently, when his lack of business experience landed him in trouble, he was offered sympathy but no practical help.

His family believe that he was finally bowled over by his own enthusiasm, in that he tried to do too many things. Had he confined himself simply to making films his independent career might have survived, instead of ending in humiliation in the cells of Brixton Prison.

With the outbreak of the Great War, Arthur Melbourne-Cooper announced that he was going to France as a newsreel cameraman, but bowed to the pleas of his wife to put his home and family first; instead, he spent the war years inspecting shells at a munitions factory in Luton. Later he took his family to Southend, where he spent a few years working as a still photographer, and then moved North to spend the rest of his working life making advertising films for a Blackpool company. He retired to the village of Coton, near Cambridge, just before the Second World War, and died in 1961 at the age of 87.

Arthur Melbourne-Cooper did not die in complete obscurity. In the 1950s his daughter Audrey (a baby in the year the family was evicted from its home in St Albans) began what has turned out to be a twenty-year quest to find the evidence that would convince historians that her father's name should be included among the pioneers of the British film industry; searching for clips of his early films, discovering old documents and records in newspaper and museum archives. A short while before her father's death she had discovered sufficient material to mount an exhibition in St Albans, held, appropriately, in the foyer of the Odeon Cinema which now stands on the site of the old Alpha Studios. Arthur Melbourne-Cooper returned briefly to the limelight as a guest-of-honour.

It is only since his death that much more evidence has come to light with the result that film historians and reference books are beginning, at last, to include the name of Melbourne-Cooper in their list of British cinema pioneers—acknowledging in particular his work on animation and his development of the cinema as a place of entertainment in its own right.

13

A DISASTER—THE PIONEER AVIATORS

Captain Patrick Hamilton took his fragile wooden flying machine into the air from a field near Wallingford in Berkshire shortly after 0600 hours on a gusty September morning in 1912. Flying conditions were not ideal but they were not the worst the aviator had encountered. Captain Hamilton was not alone; sitting muffled up in the wicker seat in front of him was Lieutenant Atholl Wyness-Stuart, his observer, and in a second aircraft just behind, was Hamilton's flight commander, Major Brooke Popham. Three Army officers who, fascinated by the exciting prospects of powered flight, had left their regiments to join the fledgling ranks of the Royal Flying Corps.

Neither pilot had held a licence for much more than a year and Hamilton had already had a narrow escape from death while flying in America, when his aircraft crashed after being sucked into an air pocket. In fact, the three men were flying at a time when there was still much to be learned about aviation and when many still held doubts about its potential. Since there was as yet no aeronautical language, motoring terms were frequently applied to these new vehicles of the air. The control column was 'the steering wheel', the metal engine casing or cowling was 'the bonnet' and airfields were known, daintily, as 'alighting grounds'. The aviators had no standard flying kit beyond an assortment of leather coats and jerkins, breeches and leather caps which had been designed originally for the pioneer motorists and motorcyclists. Nevertheless, on that Friday morning of 6th September 1912, the three men were on an important

The front page of The *Daily Mirror* of 7th September, 1912—devoted entirely to a picture of the wreckage of Captain Hamilton's Deperdussin monoplane and showing the buckled propellor in the foreground. The Graveley air disaster, the first in which airmen were killed while flying on active service, was a major news story throughout much of the Western world.

military mission, the outcome of which was awaited with great interest by the generals in Whitehall.

Although it was not until the 1914–18 war that these early aircraft were developed into proper fighting machines, the War Office had recognised their possible usefulness as a means of aerial observation, replacing the balloons and baskets and man-lifting kites used during the Boer War. Preliminary trials on Salisbury Plain a few weeks earlier had proved that aircraft could be used to great advantage to spot enemy positions and troop movements and to drop messages to their own troops in the forward lines. Now the time had come to test these 'air scouts' and their flying machines in a large-scale battle

The East of England Army Manoeuvres of 1912 caused great excitement among the civilian population—particularly in North Hertfordshire, where a meadow near Willian was taken over by the Royal Flying Corps as an 'alighting ground' for their aircraft.

134

situation. This was the mission of the three aviators as their little aircraft set off on a north-easterly course for the fifty-mile flight to North Hertfordshire and the war games.

The Army manoeuvres taking place in eastern England that autumn had been organised on an impressive scale. There were 75,000 regular soldiers and reservists taking part in a mock battle in which Blue Force was defending London against the Red Force invaders who had landed on the east coast. Captain Hamilton and Major Brooke Popham were on reconnaissance for the defenders. As their aircraft reached the Hertfordshire border the three men waved and Brooke Popham in his faster bi-plane broke away to make for his own reconnaissance area. That moment was the last time he saw his two colleagues alive. When he touched down at the R.F.C. rendezvous point at Willian, near Hitchin, later that morning, he learned that Captain Hamilton and Lieutenant Wyness-Stuart were lying dead beneath the wreckage of their aircraft, barely a mile away.

Another part of the Royal Flying Corps' temporary airfield at Willian with curious visitors, many of whom had never seen an aeroplane at close-quarters before.

To the people of North Hertfordshire, flying machines were still very much a cause of wonder and excitement; when one passed overhead, which was rarely, work stopped, housewives ran to their windows and small boys jumped on their bicycles to pedal off furiously in vain pursuit. Consequently, when Captain Hamilton brought his Deperdussin monoplane over Stevenage and began his descent over the villages towards the Willian alighting ground, hundreds of eyes were upon him. There were many, therefore, who witnessed with horror the deaths of the two men. Because there were so many witnesses it was some time before a full and accurate picture of the last moments of the Deperdussin and its crew was completed.

Nearly all estimated that the aircraft was at about six hundred feet when the trouble began. Some claimed to have seen one of the aviators fall from the aircraft to his death some time before the machine began its final dive. One said it 'plummeted to earth like a dart', another that it 'fluttered to the ground like a bird shot on the wing'. However, most agreed that the 100 horse power Gnome engine, capable of producing speeds of 70 knots, was giving the pilot trouble well before the crash dive. It was clear, too, that—for some reason—the port wing folded and collapsed while the pilot, his engine having cut out, was desperately trying to reduce height for an emergency landing at Willian. Instead, his aircraft virtually disintegrated in mid-air and fell several hundred feet to plunge into a thick hedge at the bottom of a meadow belonging to Mr Walter Brett, landlord of the *George and Dragon* public house at Graveley. 'I saw the aircraft wobbling about,' Mr Brett was to tell the coroner later. 'It dipped and then came a report like a gun. Then the aircraft seemed to collapse altogether. I was too horrified to look any more . . . I ran down and found the officers lying with the machine on top of them.' Both had died immediately upon impact.

A unique contemporary photograph of the Deperdussin monoplane piloted by Captain Hamilton. There were no special aviation clothing and his helmet consists simply of a leather cap worn in reverse. This photograph shows why so many witnesses talked of it resembling a bird.
(*Flight* magazine)

While villagers and servicemen were working to remove the bodies from the wreckage, news of the sensational crash spread like wildfire. Sightseers came from miles around, lured by the fascinating horror of this new kind of disaster. They saw the shrouded bodies carried to the horse-drawn ambulance that conveyed them to a mortuary next to St Saviour's Church in Hitchin. Some began searching the crash area and making off with pieces of the wreckage as souvenirs; the steering wheel of the Deperdussin eventually vanished this way and the curio-hunters almost prevented the investigators from discovering the cause of the crash—almost, but not quite.

137

Fortunately it was an official who found the small length of connecting rod, fractured at both ends, lying two hundred yards from where most of the Deperdussin had fallen. Thus, at the inquest, Hamilton's flight commander and the works manager of British Deperdussin were between them able to supply enough evidence for the jury to be satisfied that it was a mechanical fault and not pilot error or bad flying conditions that had caused the crash. Speculation before the inquest had suggested that with the wind that day gusting up to 40 knots, it had been too dangerous for the aviators and that they should never have taken off; but Major Brooke Popham said both Captain Hamilton and his aircraft had flown safely in far worse conditions than had existed that Friday.

Both he and Mr Fritz Koolhoven, of British Deperdussin, agreed that the cause of the crash was the fracture of the connecting rod, used to operate the exhaust valves of the engine. Having broken away, the rod thrashed about inside for several minutes eventually causing a large section of the engine bonnet to break away; this, in turn, flew back, cutting through one of the main wire struts supporting the port wing. The wing then began to vibrate violently and it was only a matter of minutes before the wooden structure folded and collapsed completely. 'After such a breakage,' Mr Koolhoven commented, 'it would be quite impossible to fly the machine.'

Superintendent George Reed, head of the Hitchin Police division, confirmed that a large piece of the engine bonnet was found three hundred yards from the crash point, adding that it was almost certainly this big object falling through the air just prior to the crash dive which led some witnesses to assume mistakenly that one of the airmen had fallen out. Major Brooke Popham revealed the irony that the aeroplane in which the two officers died had, only a few weeks earlier, won a £2,000 prize when flown by a Frenchman during the trials and competitions on Salisbury Plain. Captain Hamilton, he said, had flown

The Daily Mirror

THE MORNING JOURNAL WITH THE SECOND LARGEST NET SALE.

No. 2,773.   THURSDAY, SEPTEMBER 12, 1912   One Halfpenny.

THE SERVICES' TRIBUTE TO TWO HEROIC ARMY AIRMEN: IMPRESSIVE SCENES AT THE FUNERAL OF CAPTAIN HAMILTON AND LIEUTENANT WYNESS-STUART.

Crowds lined the streets of Hitchin yesterday, when the bodies of Captain Hamilton and Lieutenant Wyness-Stuart, the two Army officers who lost their lives in Friday's aeroplane disaster, were removed from the mortuary to the railway station for conveyance to their respective burial places at Hythe, Kent, and Wells, Somerset. At Oxford the inquest was held on Second-Lieutenant Hotchkiss and Lieutenant Bettington, the two officers who also laid down their lives in the execution of their duty. (1) Officers of the Naval Flying School saluting as the coffins pass by. (2) The gun-carriage on which the coffins were placed. That bearing the remains of Captain Hamilton is seen in the foreground. They were followed by a military escort, which included Regulars, Yeomanry and Territorials. The portraits are of Captain Hamilton, who is wearing an airman's hat, and Lieutenant Wyness-Stuart.—(*Daily Mirror* and C.N.)

There was similar national news coverage of the hero's funeral accorded the two dead aviators at Hitchin the following week. After the service, gun-carriages bore the coffins to the railway station from where they were taken to the airmen's home towns for private burial.

139

this machine for only three hours, but was used to similar machines. The jury returned a verdict of accidental death and paid tribute to the valour of the aviators. Patrick Hamilton and Atholl Wyness-Stuart were the first servicemen to die in a military aircraft while flying under military orders—the first fliers to die on active service. Their deaths were sadly the prelude to a number of disasters which clouded the first year of the Royal Flying Corps. A week later, two more colleagues taking part in the manoeuvres, Lieutenant E. H. Hotchkiss and Lieutenant C. A. Bettington, died in a similar crash near Oxford.

It was, however, the Graveley air disaster which brought home to the public with brutal suddenness the fact that the young men pioneering military aviation were engaged in an occupation that contained far more danger than glamour. Inevitably Hamilton and Wyness-Stuart, who were both aged 30, were accorded a hero's funeral. Hundreds of townspeople and villagers turned up for the service at St Saviour's Church, but since it was completely filled by family mourners and members of the Armed Services, they could only stand outside in silence, hoping to catch a few words of the eloquent tributes and the hymn that had been composed especially for the event:

> 'Direct with thine all-seeing eye
> Watch each dread journey through the sky;
> Through every storm and danger zone,
> Bring each brave pilot safely home.'

The airmens' coffins, borne by comrades of the Royal Flying Corps, were carried out to the gun-carriages; a military band, playing a funeral lament, led the cortege to Hitchin railway station past crowds lining the road ten deep in places. From Hitchin, the coffins were taken to different parts of England for private burial—Captain

Part of the large crowd which witnessed the unveiling of the memorial to Captain Hamilton and Lieutenant Wyness-Stuart on the roadside near Graveley, close to where they crashed.

Hamilton's, at his mother's request, to Hythe in Kent, Lieutenant Wyness-Stuart's, accompanied by his young widow, to Wells in Somerset. That week in Hitchin a memorial fund was opened and a stone-mason put to work, and in the last week of September a large crowd gathered once again near the field where the Deperdussin had crashed. The small granite obelisk, bearing the names of the aviators, was erected—not in the meadow where they had died—but half a mile away by the side of the road that runs between Willian and Wymondley. Captain Hamilton's mother laid a wreath of chrysanthemums upon it and his flight commander made a short speech.

'Some people,' said Major Brooke Popham, 'may think a memorial stone a waste of money and that it would have been more profitable to give it to the hospital or some local charity. I beg to differ. We should be a poor nation without recollections of noble deeds and heroic deaths to inspire us. The careless child and the weary wayfarer will pass along this road, look at this stone, read this inscription and realise that they, too, have a duty to perform. They will know that patriotism is not an empty word and that Englishmen are still ready to lay down their lives in the service of their country.'

Two years later, events in Europe proved only too well how right the major was.